To Kathleen —

Thank you for your interest and support of my work — It's delightful to get to see you again —

Best wishes in your development as an art therapist — Please keep in touch —

Love,

Carol

Telling
Without Talking

Art as a Window
into the World of
Multiple Personality

Barry M. Cohen and Carol Thayer Cox

W. W. Norton & Company   New York   London

The authors and publisher recommend that psychiatric diagnosis be based on the expertise of a mental health professional who is trained and licensed. In no way should the contents of this book be considered medical advice regarding diagnosis or treatment of multiple personality or dissociative identity disorder. Further, this text is not intended as a substitute for graduate level art therapy training.

The authors express gratitude for permission to reprint the following copyrighted material:

Excerpts from *Imagery and Visual Expression in Therapy* by Vija Bergs Lusebrink. Figures 4.5 and 4.6. Copyright © 1990, by Plenum, New York, NY.
Excerpts from *Multiple Personality Disorder from the Inside Out*, edited by Barry M. Cohen, Esther Giller, and Lynn W. Copyright © 1991, Sidran Press, Lutherville, MD.

A Norton Professional Book

Library of Congress Cataloging-in-Publication Data
Cohen, Barry M.
        Telling without talking : art as a window into the world
of multiple personality / Barry M. Cohen, Carol Thayer Cox.
        p . cm.
        "A Norton professional book."
        Includes bibliographical references.
        ISBN 0-393-70196-4
        1 . Multiple personality.   2 . Art therapy.   I . Cox, Carol Thayer.
II . Title.
RC569.5.M8C64   1995   95-3602 CIP
        616.85'236—dc20

W. W. Norton & Company, Inc., 500 Fifth Avenue, New York, NY 10110
W. W. Norton & Company, Ltd., 10 Coptic Street, London WC1A 1PU

1   2   3   4   5   6   7   8   9   0

To Anne and Jerry

for their patience

and support

Foreword

Cohen and Cox have produced a book that makes several original contributions to the field. Their overview of multiple personality/dissociative identity disorder (DID) is succinct and scholarly, and sets the stage for the main body of the book. The drawings are carefully chosen to illustrate specific points and themes, and the textual discussion of the artwork is very helpful in guiding and orienting the reader.

The authors have produced a comprehensive system for identifying DID through the systematic examination of artwork. Their method is objective, operationalized, and transmissible, which means it can be taught and learned, and does not rely on intuition, charisma, or personal characteristics of the authors. In this sense, the system could be compared to the Exner system for scoring the Rorschach, in that it brings objectivity to what would otherwise be merely impressionistic. The Cohen and Cox system is also like the objective methods of graphologists who analyze measurable characteristics of hand-written language, as opposed to making "literary" or symbolic interpretations based on untestable theory.

The method presented in *Telling Without Talking* might be incorporated into formal inter-rater reliability studies in the following way: A clinical population such as inpatients on a chemical dependency unit could be interviewed independently by a team of interviewers. The population would include individuals with no dissociative disorders, ones with DID, and ones with non-DID dissociative disorders. The vast majority or all of the dissociative disorders would be undiagnosed clinically, so interviewers would truly be blind to the diagnostic status of the subjects. One interviewer would administer a structured interview for diagnosing dissociative disorders, the Dissociative Disorders Interview Schedule; a second would administer the Structured Clinical Interview for DSM-IV Dissociative Disorders; a third would evaluate subjects' artwork; and a fourth would do clinical diagnostic interviews.

I predict that, when the inter-rater agreements of the various combinations of the four diagnostic methods were compared, analysis of artwork to make the diagnosis of DID would perform well. Cohen and Cox have developed a method of making DID diagnoses from artwork that is scientifically testable—this is a remarkable achievement. Of course, artwork cannot be used as the sole diagnostic test, any more than the Rorschach can be used properly in isolation from the clinical history and findings. The authors point out that no one should make psychiatric diagnoses based solely on artwork.

The second major aspect of their work is that it provides a method for analysis of artwork that avoids projection of meaning onto the artwork by the observer. The method can be learned and utilized by professionals who are not trained art therapists, though of course one would expect greater accuracy and richness of analysis from experienced art therapists. At the same time that it provides consistency and objectivity, Cohen and Cox's method fosters and allows the "art" of art therapy—this is evident from the commentary in the text, which for me makes the drawings richer and deeper.

The pictures themselves are profound and moving. I have watched the authors present slides of DID artwork, and have always been amazed and impressed by the drawings, but this selection is particularly outstanding for its depth and range. *Telling Without Talking* is an important contribution to the field of dissociative disorders, and to the mental health field as a whole.

Colin A. Ross, M.D.

Foreword

As an art therapist who, like others, has unexpectedly stumbled upon multiple personalities in some of my patients, I am most grateful for this book. The title, *Telling Without Talking*, is poignantly apt, because one of the reasons for dissociative identity disorders is the injunction *not* to tell. Since abused children are usually threatened with further harm if they *do* tell, they understandably have a very hard time talking about what happened to them. Most often, the amnesia that accompanies a dissociated state during trauma shields the adult survivor from conscious recollection. Yet, in order to be free of inner torment, the individual *must* find a way to tell a therapist—someone who can help her to understand and overcome the reality that was so unthinkable—and therefore indigestible—at the time it happened.

This telling—in which talking is forbidden—often speaks in the language of the body, or through other inarticulate symptoms. Such messages also may be expressed through unbidden mental imagery, intrusive thoughts that are usually both disturbing and puzzling. When graphic media are available, visual messages can be deciphered in doodles or art expressions. These clues may indeed be the most vivid and accessible evidence of an unremembered trauma. Given increased awareness of this not-so-rare disorder, a book that helps therapists to read and understand the particular language of art is both timely and welcome. It should be read by both "talk" therapists and art therapists alike, since either may receive such messages from their patients.

Like those psychiatrists who developed the DSM classifications, the art therapists who wrote this book have tried throughout to be descriptive, proposing what they call an "integrative method" to analyze art products. Having read and used many different attempts at the classification of visual art—by experimental and clinical psychologists, as well as by art therapists and art educators—I am delighted by the breadth and depth of the authors' approach. While I have not yet utilized their system, the fact that it deals with all aspects of a creative product in a sophisticated fashion is itself noteworthy.

It would appear, moreover, that the authors have found, in the art of patients with this disorder, visual analogs of the mental processes that characterize the disability itself. Some, like system pictures, represent elements of the multiple's inner world, while others, like chaos pictures, reflect its dynamic phenomenology. It is to be hoped that this way of looking will facilitate differential diagnosis and effective therapy for many individuals. Because imagery is indeed the language of the unconscious, this perspective may even enable practitioners to achieve a deeper understanding of the disorder itself.

It is a pleasure to read such a thoughtful attempt at classification and understanding. There is always a danger that those messages encoded in visual art will be either ignored as irrelevant, or—worse yet—misunderstood and misused. It is far too easy for any clinician to project his or her own ideas and feelings onto patient art. Art therapists, while wonderfully sensitive to image language, need to be carefully trained to see as objectively as possible. This is probably even more true for non-artist clinicians, who may also be more likely to receive such expressive offerings.

I hope that this book will help all of us to value and to better understand graphic communications by those who suffer from dissociative disorders. I hope too that it will increase awareness—among therapists of all sorts—of the value of art expression for severely traumatized patients. They deserve to have available to them as many avenues of expression as we can possibly provide, so that their buried and toxic tales can finally be safely told.

Judith A. Rubin, Ph.D., ATR
Faculty, Department of Psychiatry, University of Pittsburgh
Faculty, Pittsburgh Psychoanalytic Institute

Contents

Acknowledgments

To those who have contributed their creative productions to this book—and the hundreds who could not—we offer our sincere thanks. Therapists and interns who willingly took time to gather pictures and negotiate permissions from their clients for us are: Theresa Kress, Mary-Michola Barnes, Anne Mills, Delores Dungee-Anderson, Stephanie Natter, and Suzanne DesMarais. Gretchen Flock and Sue and Michael Mills were the first to read our years' work and assist in the editing process. David Cox deftly created tables and figures that concretize our new approach. Mary Strigari helped us at both ends of our project with our initial proposal as well as our cover design. Our dear friends and colleagues, art therapists Anne Mills and Barbara Sobol, served as our intellectual sounding boards, loaned us a few ideas, and provided invaluable readings of our manuscript with their unparalleled signature critiques. Members of our families, close friends, and our colleagues at THE CENTER: Post-Traumatic & Dissociative Disorders Program and The George Washington University Graduate Art Therapy Program are to be hailed for their support, interest, and forbearance during periods of absence or stress. To the esteemed faculty members of the Eastern Regional Conference on Abuse, Trauma, and Dissociation, who have (perhaps unknowingly) served as our mentors and source of ongoing inspiration in this difficult work, we acknowledge our debt. Susan B. Munro, our editor at Norton, has graciously and skillfully helped us to excise all irrelevance, obfuscation, and defensiveness from our text; we thank her for helping us to communicate our ideas more clearly. Very special thanks to Lisa D. Moore, who personally transcribed every word of our manuscript (probably one of the last in the modern world to be completely hand-written) from the illegible page to the word processor. For two years, she transcribed our copy in a good humored and unflappable manner. Finally, we owe thanks to our mentors, pioneers in the synthesis of art and psychotherapy, for constructing a foundation of theory upon which we have attempted to build, and for encouraging our endeavors.

Terminology Used in this Book

MPD ■ DID

The diagnostic category called multiple personality disorder (MPD) has recently been changed to dissociative identity disorder (DID) (American Psychiatric Association, 1994). It will undoubtedly be some years before nonspecialists adjust to the new nomenclature, and for this reason we have used the terms interchangeably. Likewise, terms such as **multiplicity**, **dissociative**, and **post-traumatic dissociation** are used to identify members of this population and their symptomatology.

alter personality ■ alter ■ part-self ■ part of self ■ ego state ■ aspect

All refer to the entities that comprise the overall personality of the person with MPD.

client ■ patient ■ artist ■ maker ■ creator

These terms, used interchangeably, pertain to the person in treatment who is making the artwork. Additionally, the feminine gender is always used, since nearly all those whose art is reproduced in this book are women.

picture ■ artwork ■ production ■ drawing ■ art

The images and expressions created to graphically communicate thoughts, feelings, and experiences. All of the examples selected for this book were created spontaneously (no directions given), unless otherwise noted.

Terminology from the disciplines of art and psychology that may not be familiar to the reader can be found in the glossary.

Art is the meeting ground of
the inner and outer worlds.
— Elinor Ulman

Art does not render what is visible,
it renders visible.
— Paul Klee

Preface

In 1987, therapists like us had just begun to get used to the notion that half or more of our clients were reporting abuse histories—but multiple personality? By that time, nearly everybody had seen the film in which Sybil, an extraordinary woman with that diagnosis was given a brilliant course of treatment by Dr. Cornelia Wilbur (portrayed by Joanne Woodward). Many of us had heard of this allegedly rare disorder only via the book and film *The Three Faces of Eve*, which was based on the life of Christine Sizemore (another remarkable woman), also portrayed by Joanne Woodward. We never believed we would actually encounter a multiple personality in our practices. But we did; we met many. It cannot be overstated how rapidly this client population seemed to enter our awareness and our offices. Of course, they had been there all along.

One of the many things that distinguishes people diagnosed with MPD from others who suffer from severe psychiatric disturbances is that they have galvanized, educated, and otherwise effected networking among their therapists. This is how our book came to be. In 1987 a woman (whom we call "Cara") suggested that her current art therapist (Barry) speak with her previous art therapist (Carol) regarding her artwork and her new diagnosis of MPD. Already acquainted, we were intrigued with the possibility of comparing portfolios of Cara's artwork.

Our mutual interest in understanding both the human need for artmaking and the wide-ranging benefits of creativity has led us into a professional collaboration that, boxes of pictures and bags of snack food later, has resulted in this book.

During the first couple of years we focused on talking with and learning from Cara, learning from others diagnosed with MPD in art therapy, and talking among our (relatively few) colleagues in this multidisciplinary field. The second year marked the initial development of the ten category model, its introduction at professional conferences, and its publication in the journal Dissociation (Cohen & Cox, 1989). Ongoing review of artwork made by Cara continued (the combined portfolio grew to nearly 1,000 pieces); in addition, we collected hundreds of pictures by dozens of MPD patients on a specialty unit, and conducted a study comparing the art of abused children with the art of adult MPD patients (Cohen, Cox, Mills, & Sobol, 1990). By 1991 we had summoned the chutzpah to pitch a book proposal; research with the Diagnostic Drawing Series (Mills & Cohen, 1993) and the Child Diagnostic Drawing Series (Sobol & Cox, 1992) and the publication of *Multiple Personality Disorder from the Inside Out* (Cohen, Giller, & W., 1991) also took place that year. It required the entire fifth year of our collaboration to sort through, categorize, and make slides from a library of thousands of pictures and to obtain permission for their publication. During the next year we developed our integrative method, while attempting to meet the deadline for our overdue manuscript. Entering year seven, we thought we had learned something about communication and collaboration. The most arduous phase in the production of this book was that last year, however, when our model was given the litmus test of usability. Each picture was reexamined in depth, and those deemed good teaching examples were organized into the manuscript. Stepping up our writing schedules, the final pieces began to fall into place at long last.

During the process we realized that all clinicians, generalists and specialists alike, need guidelines for the prudent use of art by patients with dissociative identity disorder (DID) in therapy (see also Frye & Gannon, 1993), especially those who were appropriating techniques from art therapy without availing themselves of the training necessary to practice it as a discipline. This book has several goals:

- to provide an illustrated overview of dissociative identity disorder,

■ to introduce the ten category model for adjunctive diagnostic use and
enhancement of communication in therapy,

■ and to create a primer of visual literacy for understanding clients'
therapeutic artwork.

There are many different ways of working with visual images in therapy.
This approach is intended to contribute to the differential diagnosis of DID,
augmenting a thorough history, medical evaluation, and interview. *In no way
does this book address guidelines for the clinical practice of art therapy with
DID or any other clients.* When art enters therapy, the role of the therapist
is that of observer and listener and the better part of professionalism is
discretion.

Many of the articulate and heartfelt drawings, paintings, and collages
in this book serve as testaments to their makers' childhood ordeals. To
accomplish our objectives we have chosen images that describe the full range
of vicissitudes and express the various responses common to those who live
with dissociative identity disorder (formerly MPD). Since psychotherapists and
other helping professionals who work with post-traumatic dissociative clients
must pass through this difficult territory to help clients heal, we have not
censored this material; *however, readers who may themselves have histories of
abuse, as well as those who are sensitive to material of a provocative sexual
or violent nature, are advised to proceed cautiously in viewing and reading
this book.*

The field has developed quickly since we began our collaboration. The
publication of several important books (Boon & Draijer, 1993; Kluft & Fine,
1993; Loewenstein, 1991; Putnam, 1989; Ross, 1989), a plethora of articles
about MPD (see the exhaustive bibliography by Goettman, Greaves, & Coons,
1994), instruments for detecting core dissociative symptoms (Bernstein &
Putnam, 1986; Carlson & Putnam, 1993; Ross, Heber, Norton, Anderson,
Anderson, & Barchet, 1989; Steinberg, Rounsaville, & Cicchetti, 1990),
and the proliferation of training conferences have enabled even geographically
isolated practitioners to make the diagnosis of DID in much less than the
six or seven years in the mental health system cited in two research studies
(Putnam, Guroff, Silberman, Barban, & Post, 1986; Rivera, 1991). It is our
hope that this book will contribute to this progress.

Art is an adaptive tool by which
we master forces in the
environment for survival.
– Mihaly Csikszentmihalyi

Introduction

Multiple personality disorder is rooted in the secrecy surrounding prolonged and severe physical, sexual, and emotional abuse and/or neglect starting in early childhood. The patient in treatment is typically eager to sustain that secrecy at almost any cost; thus discussing abuse amounts to a violation of the self-protective vows made by the victim in response to the abuser's threats. For those patients who are aware of the connection between trauma and dissociation, to reveal multiplicity is to signal the existence of an abuse history. The intense skepticism regarding this disorder in parts of the professional community (Aldridge-Morris, 1989; Dell, 1988; Mersky, 1992) and the fear of people with severe mental disorders in contemporary society further compound the reluctance to tell. To complicate the matter, individuals with MPD manifest symptomatology that parallels and mimics a wide variety of other disorders, including, but not limited to, depression, mood swings, headaches and numerous somatic concerns, interpersonal difficulties, sexual dysfunctions, pseudo-seizures, flashbacks, memory loss, hearing voices, and chronic suicidality (Coons, 1984).

Some patients keep the knowledge of their own abuse and multiplicity secret even from themselves, partially due to the oaths of silence exacted by their perpetrators. Because they are not sure whether "don't tell" extends to picture-making or not, drawing the memories and pain is fraught with anxiety based on cues from both outside and within. Fortunately, clients whose memories are still locked in strongboxes of dissociation as well as those who remember but are ambivalent about telling find one quality in art that allows them the best of all worlds.

Coding is an inherent benefit of symbolic expression through art, due largely to the phenomenon of multileveledness (see Chapter 1). Coding allows the patient to reveal information in a drawing while simultaneously camouflaging it from the viewer or herself (Cohen & Cox, 1989). This is achieved by the intentional or unintentional use of images that look like, are substituted for, or are camouflaged versions of a particular referent. For instance, mountains are convenient stand-ins for buttocks in drawings about abuse, and intrusive images are typically added as lightning bolts or trees. Thus, dissociated and repressed material, some of which is stored in memory as visual images, can be released to consciousness and expressed through art (Cohen, in press).

Because art is a natural and nonthreatening way for children to communicate, drawing pictures allows the abused child to assert control and have something to call her own. In adulthood, art provides parts of the self that were sworn to secrecy during childhood with a way of telling their stories. Intense affects such as rage and grief can be released and explored through art by people who previously had to dissociate feelings in order to cope with them. Thus, art becomes an important source of information about early life and a resource for communication and connection with others. For the person diagnosed with MPD, communication among alter personalities in a newly charted system can also be facilitated through making pictures.

Art therapists are attuned to ambiguous messages in art; they can be fluent in recognizing and reading the graphic communications that characterize MPD art for several reasons. Educated in distinguishing levels of graphic development and changes in drawing style, they are skilled in detecting switches between alters and pinpointing their approximate developmental ages according to graphic norms. Art therapists are trained to look for indicators of childhood trauma or suicidality and, in perplexing cases, are often called upon to assist in making differential diagnoses through art productions (Cohen, Hammer, & Singer, 1988; Mills, Cohen, & Kijak, 1994). Further, since art therapy is a treatment modality that is appropriate for both children and adults, non-English-speaking persons, those who cannot read or speak, the overintellectualized, learning impaired, blind, or affectively overwhelmed, it easily accommodates the challenges of treating multiple personality disorder and the complex multiple personality system.

In our experience, clients with MPD are often amazed that certain clinicians can read in their art what is actually being communicated by them about themselves and their inner worlds. Many had been attempting to communicate their sense of internal separateness, disconnection, and psychological turmoil in this way for years, only to be judged psychotic, secluded in hospitals, and subdued with medication. In art therapy, a lifeline can be cast between these survivors of severe abuse, retraumatized for years in an unknowing and unnoticing mental health care system, and the professionals who work with them.

Once alerted to the basic tasks, art therapists are able to traverse the complex territory of identifying and treating MPD in ways that further clarify issues otherwise obscured by its confusing phenomenology. Consequently, art therapy has become a better known discipline among clinicians working with dissociative disorder clients than among generalists in mental health practice.

As respect for art therapy and its clinical value rises, so do the numbers of clinicians untrained in using art therapeutically who wish to employ it with their DID clients. This is not surprising for several reasons. In our experience, people with MPD generate more creative productions than any other group of psychiatric patients; these productions are frequently brought into treatment regardless of the orientation of the therapist. Further, therapists who willingly treat individuals with MPD are often highly creative individuals. Thus, the therapist who feels comfortable with art might easily blur the boundary between her own skills and those of the trained art therapist.

Artmaking gives people with multiple personality the opportunity to tell without talking, thus opening a window into their internal worlds. The temptation to work with the art will always remain strong, since it is so compelling. Moreover, there is too much important information layered among the strata of meaning in these images to ignore. In order to enhance the competency of those therapists whose clients bring spontaneous art into treatment, this text is offered.

Telling
Without Talking

Art as a Window
into the World of
Multiple Personality

Seemingly careless and thoughtless
treatment of visual information is based
quite often on understandable ignorance;
since there is no recognition of a lack of
knowledge, there is no motivation to
acquire it.

– Janie Rhyne

Chapter 1

The Integrative Method
Making Sense of Art

A rt is usually made by the patient in psychotherapy as a release of affect and a recording of psychic or historical events. For survivors of severe childhood trauma, art provides a way to assert their existence in the world (Cohen, 1993). If it is to be used effectively in treatment, art must function as a vehicle for communication with the therapist, as well as for self-communication and self-revelation. Every picture communicates at least one message, often more. Some messages are intentional, others are unintentional; many pictures carry both. The less connected the client is with her thoughts, feelings, and experiences, the more crucial art becomes in her treatment. This is because art can carry complex communications that may not yet be fully conscious. For the nonspecialist, working with art becomes especially complex and challenging under these circumstances.

In order to work effectively with art productions in psychotherapy, clinicians must first learn to identify, describe, and interact with all aspects of a picture. Those clinicians who choose to bring art activity into therapy do best when they understand the influence of media on the picture-making process and the subsequent impact of picture-making on the progression of treatment. Further, the clinician's empathy for and intuition about the images in art expressions must be tempered by education, experience, and discipline if he or she is to use art responsibly within the context of psychotherapy.

One of our goals in writing this book is to introduce a method of looking at artwork to aid clinicians and patients in comprehending as many complex messages as possible from pictures that are brought into or made in therapy. The reader should keep in mind that each picture made by a client during treatment is a complicated unit; its highly personal meaning cannot be deduced simply from analyzing the sum of its parts. Ongoing discussion with the client about her artmaking process and product is essential in achieving a full appreciation of the picture and its message. Unfortunately, there are no simple or absolute rules for making the bridge between describing a work of art and fully understanding its meaning.

Our method of working with therapeutic art productions is based on a multileveled approach to the graphic image, which we call the "integrative method." Designed to give specialists and nonspecialists alike a systematic way of making sense of any art that is produced in the context of therapy, this method has proven especially helpful in paving a path into the confusing and mysterious pictorial realm of people with MPD.

The integrative method refers to a system for "reading" pictures in which meaning is derived through the synthesis of process, structure, and content elements. It draws upon the ideas and approaches of theorists, researchers, and clinicians from the fields of philosophy, psychology, communications, and art therapy. Our approach is rooted in the writings of Dondis (1973) delineating the building blocks of pictorial syntax, Arnheim's work on isomorphism (1974), and Kreitler and Kreitler's work on multileveledness (1972); it is influenced by Rhyne's research (1979) on the visual dynamics of mind-state drawings, as well as Kagin and Lusebrink's Expressive Therapies Continuum (1978). Although it was initially devised as a tool to be used in an early stage of therapy, we have found the integrative method to be an effective aid to assessment and treatment at all stages.

Visual Literacy   The integrative method holds as one of its primary tenets the importance of visual literacy in understanding pictorial communication. The first step towards achieving visual literacy—that is, the ability to read messages in pictures—is learning how to identify the basic components that comprise an image.

Rhyne, strongly influenced by the work of Arnheim, approached the challenge of visual literacy by studying simple line drawings depicting mind states (1979). She examined the "visual dynamics of form relationships, orientations, directed movement, spatial interactions, and kinesthetic qualities" (pp. 13-14) to ascertain meaning from their structural properties. Further, she sought commonalities among structural aspects of abstract monochromatic drawings of various mind-states. Although this aspect of Rhyne's work has played a large role in our conceptualization of the integrative method, we have built outward, level upon level, toward the comprehension of a picture's message, rather than focusing primarily upon individual properties of a picture's intrinsic markings.

Isomorphism Isomorphism, a concept that derives from gestalt psychology, refers to correspondence between an internal state and its external manifestation (Arnheim, 1974); thus, the creator's psychological state is reflected in the gestures transferred through drawing onto the page. The art process, the art product, and the practice of art therapy all have isomorphism at their core. Since the image on the page can embody energy, mood, or psychodynamics within a structure that enables the viewer to infer the internal state of the creator, interpretation and therapeutic intervention become possible. Once the isomorphic relationship between an artist and an art production is acknowledged, one may begin to elaborate on the meaning of the image in terms of its psychological implications. In the "isomorphic mirror," all aspects of the artmaking process and product reflect the artist's inner life.

Multileveledness "Multileveledness" is the quality that enables a multitude of related and contrasting meanings to be simultaneously communicated (Kreitler & Kreitler, 1972). According to this concept, every aspect of meaning in a work of art can be understood on its own. While no single aspect encompasses the sole meaning of the whole, all aspects can be integrated into a total network of meaning. This property also allows a work of art to retain its appeal over repeated examinations because it expands possibilities for interaction between the art product and the art observer. Since the observer has an innate capacity, also multileveled, for grasping meaning, communication can be understood perceptually, conceptually, and experientially. Therefore, it is possible, valuable, and often necessary to shift among points of view in order to fully grasp a picture's message.

FIGURE 1-1 **The Spectrum of Physical Properties of Two- and Three-Dimensional Media**

Approximate media properties for some two-dimensional media.

Approximate media properties for some three-dimensional media.

Imagery and Visual Expression in Therapy (p.85) by V.B.Lusebrink, 1990. New York: Plenum Publishing. Reprinted by permission.

Media and Tools

Media refer to the ingredients of artmaking (i.e., paper, pencil, paints), whose innate characteristics influence the qualities of both the process and the product. Media connect those who make art with the world of the senses; they offer "the feel of life" (Seiden, 1994). Kagin (1969) developed a model describing the impact of media qualities on artmaking called media dimension variables. She placed media on a continuum according to their physical properties, ranging from fluid to resistive; the more resistive the medium (i.e., wood or stone), the more energy required to interact with it. Resistive media reinforce the awareness of boundaries and enhance structure, hence are ego-strengthening. Fluid media (i.e., fingerpaints, clay, watercolors, chalk pastels) have great potential for formlessness and expansiveness and facilitate regression in clinical situations, especially when wet or applied without tools. Tools (i.e., brushes, scissors, chisels) are the implements that mediate between the artist's hands and the media itself (Kagin & Lusebrink, 1978; Lusebrink, 1990).

Most of the examples chosen to illustrate this book were created with graphic media (i.e., ballpoint pen, colored marker, oil pastel, crayon) on smooth paper. When the paper is textured, that is noted. The resistive qualities of graphic media offer the artist control and clarity of detail without sacrificing expressiveness, which is facilitated by the use of color. Most of these media are between the midpoint and the resistive end of the continuum. Figure 1-1, reprinted from Lusebrink's work (1990), illustrates the spectrum of two- and three-dimensional media.

Process Level

The process level encompasses two distinct enactments: (1) the making of the picture by the artist; (2) and the verbalizations about the art, including the artist's spontaneous comments and the dialogue between the observer-therapist and artist-client about the picture after it is completed. It is essential that every therapist understand the impact of media on the process of artmaking. For example, creating a collage with magazines, scissors, and glue is an utterly different process from hand sculpting wet clay (Lusebrink, 1990); to appreciate the client's experience, the therapist must be cognizant of these differences. Further, observation of the artmaking process is a refined skill that requires understanding the temporal, spatial, and behavioral aspects of the client's involvement (Rubin, 1984).

Analyzing art in order to explain its maker or predict psychiatric diagnosis would, however, be unthinkable to many. Is it sensible, advisable, or even possible to translate a drawing into spoken or written words? Can a therapist, in good conscience, use the image as an indication of psychopathology in order to categorize people? There are differing viewpoints on the complex issue of working verbally with art productions in therapy—when to interpret, how, and with which model. Other issues regarding the overlap between content and process as related to the verbal discussion of pictures made in therapy are explored later in this chapter.

Rubin (1984, p. 129) points out the especially "loaded" nature of discussing artwork with a patient, since the art is often perceived by the patient as an extension of herself. Because Rubin recognizes the value of looking at the art and learning from it, she emphasizes the importance of the therapist's knowledge base in regard to this skill. This, of course, includes knowing how to invite the patient to join in working with the image in such a way that she can also respond honestly, and not have to censor or confabulate to "satisfy" the therapist. For further description of the art therapist's requisite skill and artistry in working with pictures and patients in art therapy, the reader is directed to Lusebrink (1990), Robbins and Sibley (1976), Rubin (1978, 1984, 1987), and Schaverien (1992).

Structure Level

The structure level of a picture is comprised of its essential elements—the building blocks of pictorial composition. It is curious that this aspect of artmaking has been seriously overlooked by art therapists and psychologists alike, because structural properties of a picture provide basic information about a picture and its maker. The artmaking strategies that characterize style are the central elements of the structure level of a picture. They provide a framework and guidelines for the construction and deconstruction of artwork and convey the visual dynamics that transmit the picture's message.

Artmaking Strategies

Dondis (1973) delineates a variety of approaches to picture-making, which she calls "visual techniques." They are crucial to understanding how elements of a picture are manipulated structurally within a composition to convey meaning. We have condensed the wide variety of items proposed by Dondis, clarified definitions for those we have selected, paired them according to function, and renamed some of them. The following were most frequently seen in the pictures studied for this book:

NUMBER OF ELEMENTS
- *Simplicity* features the least number of elements necessary, with no extraneous features.
- *Complexity* makes use of many elements, creating intricacy and distracting from a central focus.

ARRANGEMENT OF ELEMENTS
- *Sequentiality* employs a series of items arranged in a successive pattern.
- *Randomness* gives the impression of disorganization through haphazard placement of elements with no resulting pattern and no regard for the whole.

CLARITY OF PRESENTATION
- *Boldness* draws attention to the image through clarity of form and directness of presentation.
- *Diffusion* uses gradation of pressure and color, and modulation of pictorial density, resulting in a soft-focused, atmospheric quality.

MANIPULATION OF IMAGES
- *Distortion* manipulates form beyond its natural state to heighten effect.

■ *Exaggeration* uses grand scale to amplify and overstate.

INTERRELATIONSHIP OF IMAGES

■ *Juxtaposition* concentrates on two or more images adjacent to one another.

■ *Symmetry* focuses on two images that are either mirror opposites or placed on opposite sides of a pictorial axis.

SPECIAL EFFECTS

■ *Movement* animates images through dynamic configurations and placement of line and shape.

■ *Dimensionality* employs perspective or manipulation of light and shadow to suggest distance, depth, or texture.

COLOR USE

■ *Monochrome* limits choice to a single color.

■ *Polychrome* includes more than one color.

When one is first looking at a drawing or painting, these categories provide a useful list of criteria for examination. They are structural elements of the picture that, when identified, can inform the viewer about particular aspects of the artist's communication.

Style

A style is a mode of expression with distinctive characteristics based on which artmaking strategies are used. Styles are also structural elements of pictures. We have condensed Dondis's (1973) styles into four classes most frequently seen in therapeutic art productions:

■ *Naturalism* treats forms, color, and space as they appear or might appear in the natural world.

■ *Elementalism* is characterized by simplicity, flatness, and iconographic generalization.

■ *Expressionism* manipulates form, color, or content through distortion, exaggeration, or the suggestion of movement.

■ *Surrealism* is typified by unexpected juxtaposition of images and irrational contexts.

Style gives the picture its attitude, whether that is cold and mechanistic, intensely compelling, or strange and disorienting.

Although several pioneer art therapists have acknowledged the importance of the structural qualities of pictures (Kramer, 1979; Kwiatkowska, 1978; Ulman & Levy, 1975), no art therapy model has been published to date that describes a practical approach to reading pictures that emphasizes their structural elements. Since art therapists represent a variety of theoretical and practical schools of thought, some might consider structure to be but one interesting aspect of pictorial communication. It is our belief that therapeutic artwork—to be clearly seen as well as understood in all its richness—must always be considered in terms of its structural elements before its multileveled content and the client's verbal associations to the art are placed in context. This approach recognizes structure as art's primary component, not simply a single aspect to consider.

Content Level

Content typically refers to the subject matter, theme, or story in a representational work of art. In an abstract work of art the content is embodied by the structural elements of the picture and their dynamic interrelationships (Rhyne, 1979), which often evoke mood. In both abstract and representational art, content contributes additional information toward the message of the picture. All these features can be used to describe the art production and explore its theme. Guiding principles for this process stem from the work of Kreitler and Kreitler (1972) and Schaverien (1992).

Symbolism

Each element in a work of art may stimulate a variety of associations in the viewer. Symbols are often used in the visual arts to communicate concepts that transcend what is concretely represented by the manifest image. Symbols can stand for meanings that range from specifically personal to universal. Different schools of thought in psychology provide parameters for the interpretation of symbols. Jung has been perhaps the single most influential theorist in regard to symbolism. His approach to symbols and their importance in our lives was popularized through *Man and His Symbols* (1964). Freud, on the other hand, will forever be known for introducing a reductive approach to symbolism, and countless cigar jokes will be told in his honor for decades to come. Hillman's archetypal psychology is a more recent development (1977); it describes a philosophy of working with imagery and symbols that encourages working with the symbol within the context and mood of the picture and not extracting the symbol for analysis. Wilson, an art therapist, has discussed symbol formation in art therapy based on ego psychology theory (1987). In our model there is no single preferred method of symbol interpretation; synthesizing information from the content, process, and structure levels to determine meaning is far more critical than attaching symbolic meaning to a particular image. The very nature of symbolization, in any event, precludes the adoption of any single meaning.

Color as Content

It is a generally accepted tenet that color correlates with affect (Birren, 1978; Kreitler & Kreitler, 1972; Schachtel, 1943). The structural properties of colors can be used by the artist to communicate mood. The hue, saturation, tone, and juxtaposition of colors can be manipulated to create a variety of dramatic effects. A person's emotional response to color can be conscious or unconscious and may derive from associations to personal experiences, influences of cultural milieu or residential locale, as well as exposure to everyday visual media (i.e., magazines, movies, television). But, in order to comprehend the full impact of color, we need to look beyond these factors.

It is widely held that colors have intrinsically symbolic meanings based on physical properties as well as archetypal significance. Thus colors have the capacity to elicit universal emotional responses beyond the personally determined ones. Volumes have been written on color symbology. Drawn from color theories in Western culture (Birren, 1978; Kellogg, 1984; Lüscher, 1969), a range of possible meanings for the three primary colors might be as follows: red (associated with blood, fire, and survival) is considered a hot, stimulating, and impulsive color that encompasses passion on a continuum ranging from happiness and love to aggression and danger; blue (associated with water, sky, and nurturance) is considered a cool, calming, and passive color reflecting introspection on a continuum ranging from security and well-being to withdrawal and depression; and yellow (associated with light, the sun, and wisdom) is considered a warm, stimulating, expansive color denoting self-actualization on a continuum from clarity and insight to inflation and mania. Similarly, a range of meanings is attributed to the secondary (violet, orange, green) as well as some tertiary (magenta, turquoise, chartreuse) colors. As with all types of symbolic images, color's meaning must be considered in all of its many aspects, from the universal to the personal and highly idiosyncratic.

Certain juxtapositions of colors are used to create tension and/or relief from tension (Kreitler & Kreitler, 1972). Many of the illustrations in this book are rendered in red and black, a color combination that connotes rage coupled with depression, the red signifying anger and the black reflecting despair (Kellogg, 1984). This combination can also suggest pain on physiological as well as psychological levels (Cox & Fleming, 1986). Color is an important vehicle for affect release and communication of feeling and is particularly useful for those people who find verbal expression difficult.

Honoring the Image

Langer (1953) coined the term "art symbol" to convey the meaning of a single work of art whose import should not be reduced to rational analysis and description. Reid (1969), who built on the work of Langer, underscored the synthesis of feeling, form, and content in a work of art, which Schaverien (1992) further developed into the concept of the "embodied image" in her explication of analytical art psychotherapy. Symbolic expression and multileveledness are hallmarks of the embodied image, graphically externalizing the inner world of the artist in ways that are not achievable by spoken language. Schaverien theorizes that art is not a "likeness" of the mental image, but emerges from the interplay between mental imagery and pictorial execution. Once externalized, the image exists in both time and space, unlike thought, memory, or fantasy. The truly integral nature of all aspects of the picture enhances its potential for meaning and fascination as an object, once created. Schaverien refers to this as "the life *in* the picture" (1992, p. 79). Although the integrative method is rooted in a somewhat deconstructive approach, Schaverien's reverence for the therapeutic art product is nonetheless compatible.

Determining Meaning

Here is an example of the steps through which you would proceed, using the integrative method, to look beyond a picture's surface. It is a brief synopsis of our approach to understanding pictures and their makers, especially when conscious access to explication of meaning by the artist is not possible.

PROCESS LEVEL: Imagine a person drawing a picture of many brightly colored balloons. Her execution of the image may be brisk and her gestures expansive, accompanied by comments of excitement. Or, while making the picture, the artist may be withdrawn and plodding, with posture that is constricted; her verbalizations might even reflect a sense of shame. Discussing the completed product with the artist would also be part of the process level.

STRUCTURE LEVEL: Since balloons are immediately identifiable as the content of the picture, one can note the use of media, and also identify the structural elements of the drawing (artmaking strategies and style). These provide a good deal of information about the picture's message. If the picture is expressionistic, for example, color may be intense and saturated, the forms irregular, and the placement random. This would be distinctly different from a naturalistic picture of pale colored, carefully drawn, uniformly shaped balloons, all in a row. Thus, the artist's psychological state is externalized and communicated through its isomorphic parallel in the art. A person with manic symptoms might draw in an expansive, expressionistic manner as described above. Conversely, a person with obsessive-compulsive tendencies might use a more constricted, controlled style.

CONTENT LEVEL: Next, one might perceive the balloons as a symbolic image representing the idea of celebration. The picture may also convey the concept of a group, for instance, of items, people, or ideas. The duality of freedom and restraint may be suggested if the balloons are depicted as floating or tethered. The fragile quality of a balloon may be a metaphor for vulnerability. Although no single association to the image fully explains the picture, synthesis of each level of the network of meaning adds to a comprehensive understanding of its message.

Figure 1-2 illustrates the integrative method for ascertaining meaning in any work of therapeutic art. It shows how the process and product of artmaking mirror the inner life of the artist; the viewer can synthesize the isomorphic reflections of these various components to grasp a picture's multileveled communication.

FIGURE 1-2   **The integrative method for determining meaning in artwork**

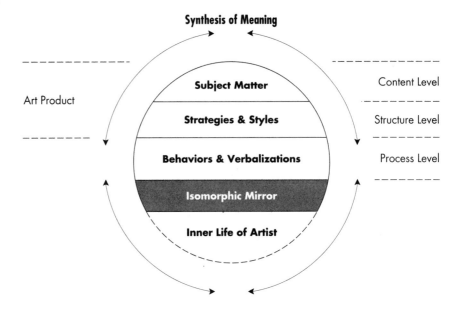

Not all pictures, however, transmit all levels of meaning to the viewer. We propose three ways to classify the extent to which a picture communicates its meaning:

■ The meaning of the picture is *obscure* when it fails to communicate clearly at any level due to extensive personal idiosyncratic coding of information.

■ The meaning of the picture is *ambiguous* when one or more of its levels are clear, while others remain obscure.

■ The meaning of the picture is *clear* when it communicates all levels of its message.

In some cases the sense of the whole work may be understood before the individual levels or parts are understood. At other times, the converse is true.

Visualizing the balloon picture again, the viewer might consider its meaning to be ambiguous based on the multileveled interplay between themes of vulnerability, freedom, and belongingness. The choice of media, structural elements such as color of the balloons, their relative size and placement on the page, and style of execution must be synthesized with these narrative elements, along with the artist's behavior and verbal comments, to achieve a multidimensional understanding of the picture; such an understanding would therefore be based on the isomorphic interaction between the artist, picture, and viewer.

The reading of pictures by the method outlined in this book is not intended as the therapist's sole source of information. Rather, it is offered as a pathway into the pictorial communication, hence to the client. Just as the art is not meant to pre-empt a thorough diagnostic assessment, the integrative method is not meant to replace thoughtful discussion with the client about her work.

Since art will be produced spontaneously during the course of treatment (especially with highly dissociative clients), it is critical that specialists and nonspecialists alike be appropriately prepared for the difficult and sensitive process of receiving its messages with the least possible contamination from projection. Despite Langer's (1953) warning that no encyclopedia can be written to provide the clinician with absolute formulas for the interpretation of these highly complex creations, our intent is to delineate basic guidelines for reading graphic communications in therapy, with the hope of facilitating this process for both patient and therapist.

Those readers interested primarily in process level aspects of artmaking and art therapy should be alerted to the fact that the focus of this text is the synthesis of meaning derived from the structure and content levels of pictures—what we refer to as the "art product." We have chosen this approach because most non-art therapists are unlikely to be present at the creation of a picture; art is typically brought into the psychotherapy session by the MPD client. Moreover, the severely traumatized person might be unable to discuss her picture due to the vicissitudes of post-traumatic dissociative amnesia, and be unable to contribute in this way to the synthesis of pictorial meaning.

The reader should keep in mind that no single picture will manifest as a textbook example and, therefore, no one should be judged clinically on the basis of a single work of art. When possible, a trained art therapist should be consulted. For a review of approaches to art therapy in the treatment of MPD, the reader is directed to the volume edited by Kluft (1993).

*Given the "iconic," visual nature of
traumatic memories, creating pictures may
represent the most effective initial
approach to these "indelible images."*
– Judith Herman

Chapter 2

The Ten Category Model
Window into the World of MPD

I t goes without saying that the client knows more about the nature of her own situation and its potential resolution than her therapist. This was especially the case during the 1980s when clinicians suddenly found themselves working with people diagnosed with multiple personality disorder. All at once thousands of therapists found themselves in a similar predicament—one of feeling deskilled—even though they had been practicing psychotherapy competently for years.

As adjunctive clinicians working in hospital and day treatment settings, art therapists did not have responsibility for primary psychotherapy with these individuals or for handling the accompanying crises. Self-harm and suicidality, differential diagnosis, and daily functioning were issues to which art therapists were attuned, but ultimately the burden of intervention fell on the primary psychotherapist or psychiatrist. As patients were increasingly admitted to hospitals in more acutely symptomatic conditions but with fewer insurance benefits, frustrated psychiatrists referred treatment refractory patients (as well as diagnostic conundrums) to expressive arts therapists. These cases, of course, consisted largely of people with histories of childhood trauma, many with undiagnosed MPD.

Art, dance, drama, music, and poetry therapists, all at the bottom of the institutional hierarchy, were given the opportunity to show what they could do with these cases. Just as the trauma model and its relation to dissociation were beginning to gel, art therapists and other mental health professionals stumbled into a field about which their clients (in certain ways) knew more than they did. Some of these patients were willing and able to communicate the basics about their inner worlds to their therapists.

Development of this Model

Cara, a patient with multiple personality disorder who had been one of a cohort of 100 in a seminal study by Putnam et al. (1986), was just such an individual. An alter personality who mentored her internal system functioned as guide and teacher to those of us who were novices in this largely uncharted territory. Her story is told in depth through her artwork in Chapter 13.

We had the extraordinary opportunity to examine more than one thousand pieces drawn by Cara over a ten-year period. These pictures spanned many hospitalizations and several diagnoses that ultimately culminated in the diagnosis of multiple personality disorder. Subsequent study of hundreds of drawings by a group of other women with MPD and discussion with them facilitated the development of a ten category model; we found that art by those with MPD naturally fell into these groupings. The identification of multiplicity through art productions thus evolved from many hours of conversation, a decade of art therapy treatment, and years of collaboration examining thousands of drawings. Originally published in a somewhat different configuration (Cohen & Cox, 1989), our ten category model was specifically conceptualized to assist therapists in the identification and diagnosis of multiple personality disorder.

We have continued to refine and revise this system of categorization as we have received feedback from other art therapists who have confirmed or questioned the existence or importance of these categories as legitimate distinctions in the art of people with MPD. The opening of an inpatient unit for the treatment of post-traumatic and dissociative disorders provided an almost inexhaustible flow of spontaneous artwork against which to test our ideas. In this way, the concepts that proved idiosyncratic to the several clients upon whose art and ideas the model had been initially developed could be separated from those that were more universal.

After verifying the viability of this model, we have found that it functions as an effective format for exploring memories, feelings, and other constantly unfolding information in the ongoing psychotherapy of MPD, as well.

Each of the following ten categories describes a type of picture in terms of its structural elements and/or theme:

■ SYSTEM pictures depict an array of individual elements forming and working as a unit that represents the current internal organization of part-selves.

■ CHAOS pictures illustrate extreme emotional or physiological distress through compositional disorder or exploding or opposing elements.

■ FRAGMENTATION pictures reflect a sense of psychic disunity and physical disconnection by the depiction of fractured or shattered elements.

■ BARRIER pictures include a structure that separates objective from subjective realities, self from environment, present from past, and ego states or alters from one another.

■ THREAT pictures employ menacing imagery to represent a warning by one or more alters of impending punishment within the system or to the body.

■ INDUCTION pictures feature primitive markings characterized by dotting, spiraling, or meandering lines; they reflect the process of going into a trance state.

■ TRANCE pictures communicate information that cannot be put into words by combining a variety of visual strategies to create scenarios which defy objective reality.

■ SWITCHING pictures concretize shifting from one ego state or personality to another as evidenced by changes in media, strategies, styles, and graphic development.

■ ABREACTION pictures graphically record aspects of repressed or dissociated memories and experiences prior to, during, or following their recall, release, and processing in psychotherapy.

■ ALERT pictures simultaneously reveal and conceal experiences of abuse, dissociation, or multiplicity by making use of the multileveledness of images.

Applying the Integrative Method

Synthesis of the ten category model with the process, structure, and content levels of pictures facilitates the use of the multilevel integrative method for the identification, exploration, and gradual understanding of therapeutic art productions by dissociative clients. The illustrations in this book are organized toward improved comprehension of meaning in the art product, which is defined in Figure 2-1. Each of the ten chapters that follows describes one of the

FIGURE 2-1

The integrative method for determining meaning in artwork by clients with dissociative identity disorder

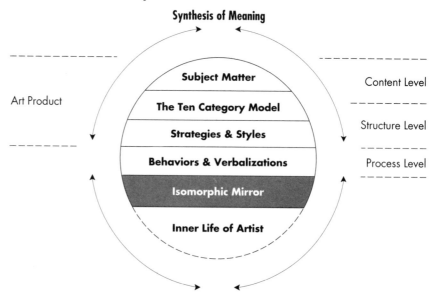

picture types in the ten category model. The category is first introduced in terms of its significance to the phenomenology of DID. Every illustration is objectively described in terms of its structural elements, including the medium, artmaking strategies, and style employed. Upon this framework are laid the subjective associations suggested by working with the picture's content. In order to establish the basic tenets of differential diagnosis through art (which includes use of the ten categories), pictorial indicators similar to those by clients with other diagnoses are discussed. When interrelated, structural and content components provide the isomorphic basis of communication between the artist and the viewer, facilitating the robust comprehension of meaning.

Our close examination of the pictures selected for publication in this book, as well as hundreds of others that were considered, has confirmed that nearly every category is associated with typical artmaking strategies and styles. Tables 2-1 and 2-2 represent these findings in detail. Readers will be introduced to a systematic method of looking at visual art that can assist in the detection of types of pictures characteristically made by people with dissociative identity disorder. Recognizing these pictures and grasping more of their ambiguous or obscure messages can create a synergy in treatment between the client, therapist, and artwork. When working with the daunting complexity of the DID system and DID art, this process can enhance therapy in a variety of ways.

TABLE 2-1 Styles seen in each category

CATEGORIES	Naturalism	Elementalism	Expressionism	Surrealism
System	X	X	X	X
Chaos			X	
Fragmentation	X	X	X	X
Barrier	X*	X	X*	X
Threat	X	X	X*	X*
Induction		X*	X	
Trance				X
Abreaction	X	X	X*	
Switching	X†	X†	X†	X†
Alert	X	X	X	X

*Most frequently seen   †In combination with other styles

TABLE 2-2 Artmaking strategies most frequently seen in each category

	Number of Elements		Arrangement of Elements		Clarity of Presentation		Manipulation of Images		Interrelationship of Images			Special Effects	Color Use	
CATEGORIES	Simplicity	Complexity	Sequentiality	Randomness	Boldness	Diffusion	Distortion	Exaggeration	Juxtaposition	Symmetry	Movement	Dimensionality	Monochrome	Polychrome
System			X						X			X		
Chaos		X		X			X	X			X			X
Fragmentation	X			X	X		X	X					X	
Barrier	X				X			X	X	X	X	X		
Threat					X				X	X	X			Red/Black
Induction				X		X					X		X	
Trance				X			X	X	X				X	
Abreaction	X				X		X	X			X			Red/Black
Switching				X	X				X					
Alert	All techniques are seen; one is not more specific to this category than any other.													

Chapter 3

System Pictures
Parts of the Self

W hile working in the all-too-fascinating realm of multiple
personality, one critical concept to keep in mind is that only
one person is with you in treatment, no matter how many
different aspects or personalities present themselves
behaviorally (Putnam, 1989; Ross, 1989). This issue is often passionately
debated by the patient with MPD throughout the course of treatment. Feelings
of disunity reinforce the conviction that the alters are actually other people; at
the same time, the patient will typically argue against her own multiplicity.
This paradoxical stance is at the heart of the disorder, fueled by internal
conflicts about the abuser, the abuse, and the societal and clinical
controversies surrounding this diagnosis.

The therapist working with MPD must always work within the system of
alter personalities to effect change. "System" refers to the interrelation among
alter personalities and other parts who inhabit the inner world of the MPD
client and who usually function on her behalf. Just as in any organization,
members may work well together at certain points in time, and not at others.
When the various parts of the MPD system are working in concert, then its
existence is rarely noticeable to the outside world. This enables individuals
with MPD to maintain a social facade of functional unity. When conflict and
chaos rule, the system is destabilized, along with the patient's functioning.

Although every MPD system is structured somewhat differently, there are
typical patterns of organization and predictable personality types within each.
For an excellent introduction to the inner cast of characters, readers are

directed to Putnam (1989) and Ross (1989). Certain alters may exert power, perform particular functions, or maintain executive control of the body at various times. These circumstances may shift and change periodically for a variety of reasons. There is no formula for predicting the machinations of MPD systems; however, with careful scrutiny by the therapist, each system will reveal its own dynamic.

Because the internal system is the central force propelling the person with multiple personality disorder through her life, pictures about it and its ongoing status are common in the productions of the MPD client. In the authors' experience, system pictures often appear before the diagnosis is made because patients frequently have an intuitive sense of their multiplicity. In some cases, alters will surreptitiously represent the system through multileveled or highly ambiguous drawings, even when the client remains consciously unaware of its existence.

Repetitions of forms or multiples of the same object (i.e., circles or eyes) and variations on a theme (i.e., candies or machine parts) are typically used to convey the idea of alters in a system picture, especially in magazine collages. Images of buildings and trees as well as groups of objects such as balloons and flowers are frequently seen visual metaphors for systems. It is not uncommon to see the system drawn representationally (consciously or not) as a group of people, usually children and adults. These pictures are often described by the patient as "friends" or "family." The most common and perhaps the least recognizable to the uninitiated viewer are the geometric configurations used to depict systems that simply look like abstract designs. They may be characterized by groupings of varied shapes such as circles or boxes and might be circumscribed by a larger shape.

Pictures of the entire system are rare because people with MPD are less likely to have complete awareness of every alter, especially in complex MPD when personalities and fragments number from several dozen to several hundred. Many pictures about the system feature particular alters, their experiences, and their vantage on the system and its politics.

FIGURE 3-1

Structure: Fine tip marker and colored pencils were used to create this picture, which juxtaposes many faces inside the looking glass of a hand-held mirror. Suspended in space against a plain background, the mirror's frame and handle are marked with jagged lines. Although the face at the right is drawn in a representational style, the remainder of the faces are stylized and somewhat surreal in their disembodied state.

Meaning: People with severe dissociative disorders frequently experience discomfort and disorientation when they look at themselves in the mirror. In many cases, they are unlikely to see a predictable reflection, due to the changeability of self-image in MPD. This picture concretizes (at a clear level of meaning) some of what is known about the patient's system of personalities, including various ages, genders, and specifics of identity. The more detailed each reflection in the mirror, the more crystallized that aspect is in consciousness. The zigzag lines covering the mirror frame remind the observer of the fragile nature of identity, particularly in this disorder.

FIGURE 3-2   **Structure:** An expressionistic drawing in charcoal depicts a group of small distorted faces randomly arranged around a central portrait, which is drawn in a naturalistic style. The image is complex and fills the page, thus avoiding any pattern. Images near the edge of the page are diffuse. Dimensionality is created by the use of chiaroscuro (light and shadow) resulting from the overlapping of the faces, particularly above and left of the portrait.

Meaning: Drawn by a patient diagnosed with MPD, the naturalistic portrait of the artist is surrounded by a myriad of alters. Faces seem to extend beyond the boundaries of the page, suggesting a limitless number of characters. The distortion in the faces helps to convey intense emotion and changeability. The density of the faces, combined with the effect of depth, suggests to the viewer that they may be packed several layers deep. There is one basic level of communication in this picture, and its meaning is clear: the patient is depicting an extensive system of personalities that are crowding and overwhelming her. The fact that they all seem to impinge on the boundaries of her head further suggests that they collectively demand her attention.

Were the picture brought into treatment by a patient not diagnosed with MPD, these descriptors would remain relevant; however, associations to the face images would require clarification. In the authors' experience, patients wishing to dissimulate their multiplicity assign vague or ambiguous meaning to such pictures. Those who remain unaware of their multiplicity may give no explanation at all.

FIGURE 3-3

Structure: A group of twenty-seven figures is depicted standing and sitting in a circle outdoors. Painted in tempera, each figure is carefully delineated, with attention to facial details as well as clothing. There is an overall sense of boldness in the execution of this naturalistic image. Outside the circle of people appear two figures; one is seated, the other is standing. Inside the circle is a transparent figure on the ground. Linear and aerial perspectives are mixed freely.

Meaning: Moving sequentially around the circle from person to person, one is struck by the variety of this group, which includes adult men and women, children, and infants. The gathering is also racially diverse. Color is an important aspect in the depiction of the clothes, as almost everyone is wearing an outfit of a different color. Placed against a rich ground of green, these colors become even more vibrant. The combination of perspectives used creates a somewhat vertiginous effect—the viewer is elevated into the sky and half the group dangle upside down, as if they were beads in a necklace. This is typical of the schematic stage of graphic development, usually seen in latency-age children. There is little else in this picture to suggest pathology. Only the upside down transparent figure gives one pause. One might see this as a picture of a contemporary family gathering or an office picnic. When dissociation is suspected in a client, however, pictures like this one help to clarify the issue of multiplicity and refer to the system of personalities.

FIGURE 3-4

Structure: Four adult and two child figures are depicted in this soft-focus group portrait, drawn in pencil. Although the central figures are clearly portrayed, the figure on the right at the rear has indistinct features; the figure at the left has none. Use of light and shadow in conjunction with the positioning of the figures creates dimensionality in this naturalistic drawing. The figures are sequentially arranged on the page, establishing a subtle pattern.

Meaning: When this drawing was brought to one of the authors, the diagnosis of MPD had been inferred by the art therapist based on several previous pictures. This image, described by the patient as "a portrait of me," confirmed our diagnostic suspicions. Although the psychiatrist was not yet ready to establish a diagnosis of multiple personality disorder, and the patient was not ready to tell her secrets, this drawing served as a clear window into the internal world of its creator. Unlike previous illustrations, there are no suggestions of unseen others in this picture. Characters are distinguished primarily by their ages. The smallest figure, seated in the lap of the girl, seems to be a doll (because of the length of its hair). Cloaked figures are somewhat typical and usually represent dark, mysterious, or unknown aspects. Faceless figures may eventually gain their features as they participate more in the patient's life and treatment. Diffusion is an apt strategy for portraying the unknown. Meaning, nonetheless, is clear in this self-portrait, despite the inability of the artist to verbalize it.

FIGURE 3-5

Structure: A husky male figure's torso, with two faces juxtaposed on its chest, is the subject of this expressionistic charcoal drawing. Distortion is evident in the elongated arms as well as the exaggerated scale of the face on the right. There is a haze of grey surrounding the figure.

Meaning: The scale of the torso juxtaposed with the fragility of the inner faces underscore the power of the figure, as does the fact that the face on the left is in the palm of the hand. Despite the formidable physical aspect of this figure, its vulnerability is suggested by the closed or covered eyes in the three faces depicted. The artist is a petite woman in her forties who has reported the sensation of being physically held by her alter personalities. Drawn to convey the role and influence of a particular male alter in her system, this picture's meaning remains ambiguous, even when the diagnosis is known. There are insufficient clues to the placement and function of the auxiliary faces with the torso to communicate their meaning. The diffusion further supports this ambiguity.

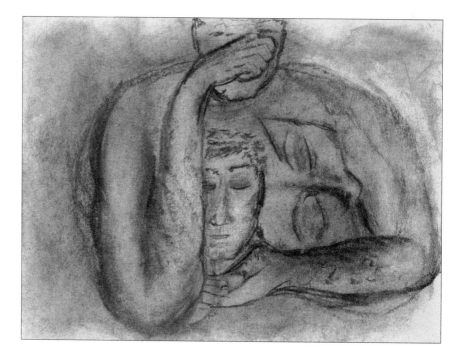

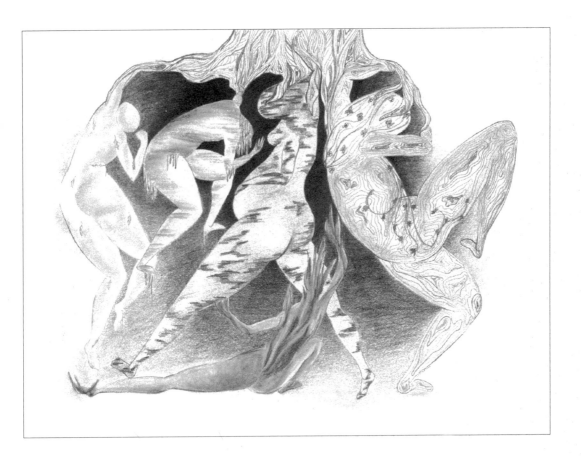

FIGURE 3-6   **Structure:** Five humanoid figures are depicted in various contorted poses. Each body has distinctive markings on its skin. Darkness accentuates the space between them. A sinuous mass tops the image, which is meticulously drawn in pencil in a surrealistic style.

Meaning: The cut-away underground view of a tree surprisingly reveals nude female bodies, twisting in the manner of a tree's root system. The decorative designs on each figure distinguish one from the other, their distorted anatomies emphasizing weightiness. The dark area behind the root-people communicates the depth of this subterranean locale, which is a metaphor for the unconscious. As noted in Figure 3-9, the tree is frequently adopted by individuals with MPD to represent aspects of self. In this case, a group of alter personalities are depicted "at the root" of the issue being explored in this picture.

FIGURE 3-7

Structure: This mixed media composition combines black marker with cut magazine pictures and features a silhouette of a tree standing against the whiteness of the page. The left branch is broken; pieces or leaves tumble to the ground. The remaining branches are topped with multicolored pointed shapes. Each branch is connected to the trunk, forming a fan-like pattern. This gestalt is further reflected in the sequentially arranged leaf formations.

Meaning: The surreal nature of this picture becomes evident to the viewer upon noticing the details in the collaged leaf system. Hundreds of tiny people comprise the crown of this tree (see detail above). Reduced in scale, they have been juxtaposed with the branches of the tree to look like leaves; they represent a system of alters. The falling leaf-people may indicate a loss of communication or cooperation within the various groupings. Of all the self-tree images included in this chapter, this one is perhaps clearest in its message of multiplicity, though its deft execution belies the complex internal world of its creator. It is difficult to imagine any other explanation for this elegant image.

CHAPTER 3

FIGURE 3-8

Structure: This simple image of a flower, its leaves and petals juxtaposed with human eyes, is an excellent introduction to the surrealistic style. Boldly drawn in pen and ink, the image stands front and center, with no unnecessary details to detract from its message. The flower's stem is segmented. Once again, overlapping of elements suggests depth, but the overall image is quite static.

Meaning: Flowers are commonly used to represent systems in the artwork of people with MPD. Flowers can be grouped, in or out of a vase, or, as in this case, the petals can carry the metaphor. Previously, eyes have been associated with the drawings of people diagnosed with paranoid schizophrenia (Dax, 1953). Although there is no comparative study to date on the respective prevalence of eyes in the artwork of these two groups, eyes in the drawings of people with MPD are typically described as representations of alters (watching from within) and abusers (observing from outside) (Spring, 1993). In this case, since the sinister stares are so unyielding in their scrutiny of the viewer, the relationship between the patient and her internal system should be carefully explored.

Although no single picture should ever be used to establish a diagnosis, ones as clear as this should strike a note of warning for the therapist of a client not diagnosed with MPD.

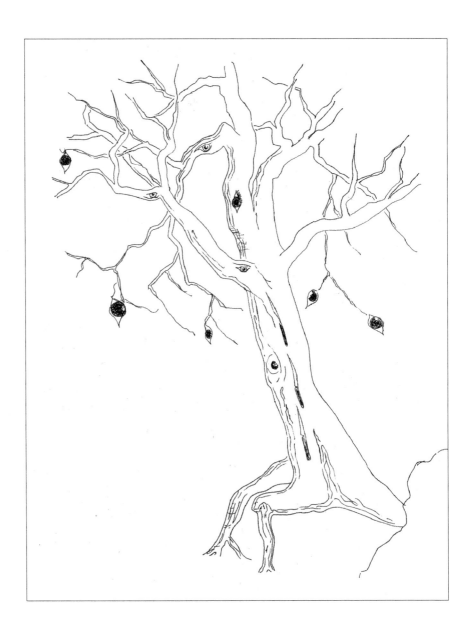

FIGURE 3-9

Structure: Drawn by the same woman who drew Figure 3-8, this pen and ink rendering of a tree suggests dimensionality and complexity in its intertwining branches. Surrealistic in style, leaves on the tree and holes in the trunk are replaced by eyes; knives are juxtaposed with the trunk; the distorted roots are exposed, one of which is connected to an indistinct shape in the lower right-hand corner of the page. There are no environmental details around the tree.

Meaning: The tree is probably the most frequent non-human image drawn to represent the self in the art of individuals diagnosed with MPD. This tree is distinguished by its relative barrenness; however, the eye-leaves are startling additions to a predictable image, which transform it into a system picture. The knives drawn up the trunk (where scarring is often seen in the tree drawings of survivors of sexual abuse) (Rankin, 1994; Torem, Gilbertson, & Light, 1990) provide another element of surprise. The anthropomorphism of the roots on the left, which resemble bent legs, and the phallic protrusion on the right, further add to the disturbing gestalt. Danger symbolized by the knives coupled with the penetration suggested by the phallic-shaped root illustrate the association between sexual trauma and self-harm for this patient. The system of eyes is ever vigilant, both on the inside and out.

CHAPTER 3

FIGURE 3-10

Structure: This naturalistic drawing of many different colored balloons is drawn in oil pastel. The balloons extend to the edges of the page with a blank space in the lower right corner. Some are colored-in fully, others are not. As with Figure 3-2, complexity and randomness create an overall busyness in this drawing, without any specific pattern. Overlapping of images establishes dimensionality.

Meaning: A large grouping of multicolored balloons floats in the picture frame without strings attached. The empty space in the lower right allows the viewer to perceive movement (without any actual depiction of motion). No color is used in this empty space to indicate context; thus the balloons may be confined in a box or a room, or in the limitless expanse of a sky. Since these untied balloons should float freely, the traffic jam image suggests either a boundary just beyond the picture frame or an infinite number of balloons.

Many aspects of this picture contribute to ambiguity of meaning. Some balloons are colored, while others are not; the balloons are untied and should be floating freely, but appear confined; they may represent either a finite or an infinite number. Various themes are raised for our consideration. Freedom, vulnerability, mobility, escape, and individuality all arise from the artist's choice of symbol: balloons. Although the artist may have intended to communicate clearly, this picture is fraught with dualities that require additional exploration. The meaning here is considered ambiguous, even when drawn by a patient with an acknowledged diagnosis of MPD. Without the benefit of the diagnosis, the multileveled aspects of its meaning would most likely be missed by the therapist and the picture disregarded completely because of its deceptively straightforward and stereotypic nature.

FIGURE 3-11

Structure: A series of tricolored markings are patterned in a triangular formation, the apex of which is a grouping of radiating lines. Each configuration is overdrawn by yellow; three are also colored over in red. Drawn in marker, in an elemental style, the entirety is circumscribed by black curlicues and red cross-hatching.

Meaning: This abstract image communicates two essential concepts—the interior grouping and the enclosure around it. The burst configuration at the top suggests physical impact, thematically reinforced by the blood-red images below. The elaborate perimeter protects and contains elements within it.

Pictures such as this one do not easily reveal their meaning. By resorting to abstraction the artist ensures ambiguity by withholding any references to the natural world. The only clues to dissociation or multiplicity are the repetitive markings, which are suggestive of a system of internal parts, and the complex boundary that surrounds them. A hierarchical organization may be seen within the grouping. Strong affect, indicated by the red—also used to signify blood in the drawings of severely traumatized patients—may be directed at these three alters. This image was drawn by a nine-year-old male personality of the same adult woman who drew Figures 3-2 and 3-5.

FIGURE 3-12

Structure: Several concentric circles are drawn predominantly in red and black chalk pastel. The numbers one through five appear within two rings of the picture in conjunction with a series of pointed forms. Brown fills the space in the center of the picture, while grey surrounds the entire image. Elementalism has been employed in this instance, featuring the artmaking strategy of simplicity. Sequentiality is also evidenced in the layered bands, numbers, and wedge forms. The directness of presentation in this picture typifies boldness.

Meaning: Despite the graphic clarity achieved by this artist, the meaning of this picture is rather difficult to determine. Before the study of art expression in MPD, art therapists would have had few clues to unlock the mystery of this rigid and static configuration. Target-like images such as this have been thought to be products of paranoid or obsessive-compulsive patients (Kellogg, 1984). Counting, a form of perseveration or ritualistic behavior, further supports these associations.

In this picture, a patient with MPD manifests the first-identified alters in her newly unfolding system. The wide black band on the outside functions as her protective barrier. The juxtaposition of red and black creates a dynamic tension between strong affect and an unyielding boundary. The haze of grey, often used by depressed individuals to depict their mood, refers to the external world. Drawn during a hospitalization, the picture obliquely portrays the sense of confinement, anger, and need for self-protection in a highly coded abstraction. Once this patient's MPD diagnosis was made, the obscure meaning of this picture shifted toward ambiguous.

Conclusion   Just as system pictures are as unique as the human beings they represent, every art style is employed in their making. Although many artmaking strategies may be used, three are particularly effective in communicating the necessary information about the system to the viewer: juxtaposition, sequentiality, and dimensionality. Juxtaposition allows images to be placed into a context in which they can function as metaphors for the system or its parts. Items that are elements of a larger whole (petals of a flower, leaves of a tree, spokes of a wheel) provide an effective format for communicating the components of a personality system. Because systems are naturally comprised of a series of parts arranged in some meaningful way, sequentiality is frequently used in composing a system picture. It is often the intent of the artist when depicting a system to convince the viewer of its authenticity. Dimensionality is the most effective strategy for achieving realism in a drawing, whether or not its subject actually hails from the visible world. Additionally, dimensionality facilitates portrayal of spatial depth necessary to accommodate the sheer volume of personality representations that comprise the average MPD system.

Meaning in system pictures tends to be highly ambiguous because of the camouflaging effect of many system configurations. Even when the viewer is alerted to the possible presence of a system picture, the meaning may remain unclear. This is primarily due to the unexplained relationship between parts of self in these pictures. While the system picture (ideally) portrays the relationships between the internal parts in varying degrees of collaboration, tensions within and external to the system stimulate conflicting thoughts, feelings, and behaviors which may, in turn, be depicted. These images are referred to as "chaos pictures" in the ten category model.

THE MIND
IN HELL

Chapter 4

Chaos Pictures
The System in Disorder

D o you remember what happened in grade school when the teacher left the room with no one in charge? Imagine that this level of confusion could erupt at any moment of your life, with no one in authority to reestablish control. Now consider the increased potential for tumult with a cast of characters that includes bawling infants, rambunctious adolescents, timid wallflowers, menacing bullies, and an array of others ranging from disoriented and dysfunctional to powerful and pernicious. What would it be like if this fracas was let loose inside your head?

For the person with dissociative identity disorder, the possibility of such internal pandemonium always exists. As mentioned earlier, the system of alter personalities can get out of balance. As each part-self spends more time in executive control of the person's thoughts and actions, it becomes easy for each and every alter personality to believe in its sense of autonomy. Once this occurs, affect intensifies and internal discord rises to intolerable levels. At such moments, the arguing, crying, badgering, and agitation can be likened to a symphony orchestra warming-up; headaches are usually manifested physiologically at these times (Braun, 1983; Ross, 1989) and their severity can be debilitating. Headaches are also commonly associated with switching phenomena. In some cases, somatic flashbacks or body memories may, in concert with severe emotional distress, be the cause of this state.

Certain patients report the cognitive confusion, affective uproar, systemic disorder, and physiological response to be debilitating to the point of functional incapacity. According to Putnam, these "internal uproars in which the personality system degenerates into a screaming mob . . . often prevent further work by overwhelming the patient with internal stimuli" (1989, p. 214). Such disturbances are frequently incited by internal discord among personalities. Typically they concern revealing versus keeping secrets, jockeying for executive control over actions, and externalizing a variety of post-traumatic conflicts within the system. Chaos can occur when switching does not or cannot occur or when switching occurs so rapidly that the system becomes completely destabilized. These behaviors are usually the result of situational psychodynamics in a dysfunctional alter personality system. Sedatives can offer a "time out" period for some patients, and this state may resolve upon awakening, with improved organization and relative calm.

The art that heralds and characterizes this internal commotion is distinctive. In its mildest form, the chaos picture can resemble the stereotypic scribble drawing in which negative spaces are filled in with colors or patterns. (Non-DID populations may use this activity to help pass time while avoiding the emotional commitment necessary to explore feelings and experiences.) When drawn by dissociative clients, the scribbles may be contained within a heavily reinforced boundary (see Figure 4-2). Drawings more easily recognized as chaotic feature dynamically drawn arrows, spirals, and lightning bolts showing energy moving inward or outward in relation to a central point (Mills & Cohen, 1993). Terms that best describe these compositions reflect their qualities of movement and force. The classic chaos picture shows an explosion, usually from the top of the head. Atomic bombs, volcanoes, and fires are images that occur again and again.

FIGURE 4-1

Structure: Movement is a key feature of this abstract chalk pastel drawing. A series of bold red spirals, dense black wedges, yellow zig-zag lines, and blue pointing arrows overlay a large red vortex. All elements appear to move at once, animated by directionality towards the edges of the page; the interplay of intense color and overall movement contribute to visual tension and exaggeration.

Meaning: No one viewing this picture would describe it as harmonious; the swirling motion propels the black shapes outward, as if in an explosion. Intense colors clash, creating a vibrant affective statement. Drawn by any psychiatric client, this expressionistic picture would be seen as reflecting the extreme chaos. When one knows that it was drawn by a client diagnosed with MPD, another level of meaning is clarified, as the conflict within the system is brought into focus. As there is behavioral decompensation in the patient, her art isomorphically reflects this dissonance.

CHAPTER 4

FIGURE 4-2

Structure: Yellow, red, and purple lines intertwine and overlap in an intricate, random fashion. They fill the space within a heavy border of black and purple densely drawn lines. The central area is punctuated by angular black markings. Certain areas of negative space are filled in with green, red, black, and purple. The image is drawn in colored marker.

Meaning: The wildly disorganized scribbles in this drawing directly convey a feeling of confusion and disorder. Although the solid shapes function as minor foci, the overall impact here is tumult. The juxtaposition of the frame (which serves as a container) with the morass of lines creates a visual and psychological tension for the viewer. Such a drawing by a psychiatric patient may suggest mania to an art therapist. The DID patient who drew this picture was most likely attempting to manage the intense turmoil experienced in this state.

FIGURE 4-3

Structure: A large face is drawn in red marker with a long broken line extending downward from the inner corner of each eye. Boldly placed across the full surface of the page, this image is complicated by the overlapping of approximately one dozen similar but smaller faces drawn in beige, grey, and black. The juxtaposition of sizes, combination of colors, and seemingly random placement of images produce a layering effect, which suggests diffusion and dimensionality; the repeated broken line extending in every direction also implies movement. This broad array of artmaking strategies produces a complex and chaotic composition.

Meaning: One is immediately struck by the number of pairs of eyes that stare out from this picture; each face frowns and cries a stream of tears. The affect in this drawing is not overwhelmingly sad; yet, there is a definite feeling of being overwhelmed. There are so many crying faces in this composition and each one can be seen through another; these transparencies result in a multidimensional composition that suggests deep space. Perseveration, transparency, and disorder are structural elements that might be associated with the artwork of a psychotic patient. On the content level, the presence of eyes might further suggest paranoia, while the crying and frowning might allude to depression. However, the affective content is not typical, for instance, of paranoid schizophrenia, nor is the compositional complexity associated with depression. The disparate use of artmaking strategies (especially movement), jumbled composition, and conflicting content, in this instance create graphic chaos, which reflects the inner world of a DID patient in distress. These characteristics also distinguish this drawing from a system picture.

FIGURE 4-4

Structure: Magazine images that comprise the complex composition of this collage are randomly placed against a background of stippled red, yellow, and orange. Central to this disorderly array of faces, body parts, and words is the cartoon "POW!" of a fist blow to the side of a head. Screaming, crying, and menacing visages are distorted by expressionistic style.

Meaning: Emotional distress is expressively depicted in the Picasso drawing at the bottom center, the woman clutching her head, the crouched nude, and the various crying figures throughout this picture. A boy with a thermometer, a bloodshot eye, a red figure with a backache, and people clutching their heads amplify, through physiological example, the experience of "brain pain." A fiery red background further heightens the affective impact of this disorderly composition. The experience of internal confusion began for this client with a headache that progressed throughout her body, immobilizing her with physical and emotional pain. The picture's content, style, strategies, and color intensify the artist's message.

FIGURE 4-5

Structure: A collage of cut bits of paper, magazine photos, and pieces of ribbon are scattered within a painted boundary of magenta. Red, yellow, and orange are slashed across the surface in a random fashion, adding to the complexity of this composition. Centrally located at the right side of the picture is the black and white photo of a young woman. Movement, saturated color, and distortion of form combine to produce an overall effect of physical and emotional release, hallmarks of expressionism.

Meaning: Strident color and a multifaceted picture plane suggest a mosaic gone haywire. The complicated and disorganized scraps and shapes burst like fireworks around the person, whose face is partially covered by red and magenta. Confusion is portrayed in an anarchic manner. The communication of a message in this mixed media work leans toward the obscure; the verve of application and saturation of color suggest mania, yet there is a condensed, tortured organization that differs from the expansiveness typically seen in the works of manic patients. After creating this collage along with another magazine picture collage (primarily of black and white images) depicting cruel scenes of abuse, the artist stated that she wished to express "the atmosphere of chaos and rage" that the adult survivor must live with in the wake of severe domestic violence.

THE MIND
IN HELL

FIGURE 4-6 **Structure:** A head, painted in the elemental style, is topped by a mass of red paint. Tiny stick figures in a variety of positions are drawn within the red; some topple over the edges of the form, along with streams of red and droplets of black. The picture is titled in the lower right: "The Mind in Hell." The image fills the page.

Meaning: Even without reading the title of this picture, the viewer's attention is drawn to the intensity bursting from this generically drawn head. Clearly something is amiss, and the blank eyes and "little people" might be glibly interpreted as hallucinatory indicators in the work of a psychotic patient. For the clinician sensitive to the part-self imagery of the dissociative client, however, a multitude of figures raises the index of suspicion regarding multiplicity. In this particular case, the distress of the psychophysiological state is evidenced by the use of color, which simultaneously represents blood, emotion, and pain.

FIGURE 4-7

Structure: Jagged lines and shapes of red, orange, and blue project upward from the top of the stylized drawing of a head. Hands are placed on the sides of the head and may be covering its eyes. This bold image floats on the page; there is no further body or environmental context in this expressionistic marker drawing.

Meaning: Blazing color and dynamically drawn shapes suggest a raging fire bursting from the head of the drawing's subject, and this person is unable to hold back the power and energy within. The simple linear drawing of face and hands is contrasted with the explosion of color. The grimace on the face signals discomfort and pain. Could this be a client with a migraine headache? Yes, and more than that, this picture reflects the chaos of an internal system of personalities in conflict drawn by a client with a severe dissociative disorder.

His head came off when everybody surrounded him in the classroom) 8/12

FIGURE 4-8   **Structure:** Colored shapes are massed around the crown of this rather realistically drawn head. Lines and bits of color suggest movement as they disengage from the design above the eyes and careen down around the ears. Drawing primarily in oil pastel, the artist has used every available color boldly above the head and subtly in the background.

Meaning: A focus on the head and the jumble of the colored-in scribble might imply psychotic ideation in this dynamic image. The internal state of the creator's mind is externalized in this drawing; it conveys confusion. The facial expression reflects a sense of passive resignation. In this chaos picture, drawn by a woman diagnosed with MPD, the emphasis is less about physical distress than on the disorganization of the system of personalities; as the client wrote at the bottom of the picture, "her head came off when everybody screamed (in technicolor)."

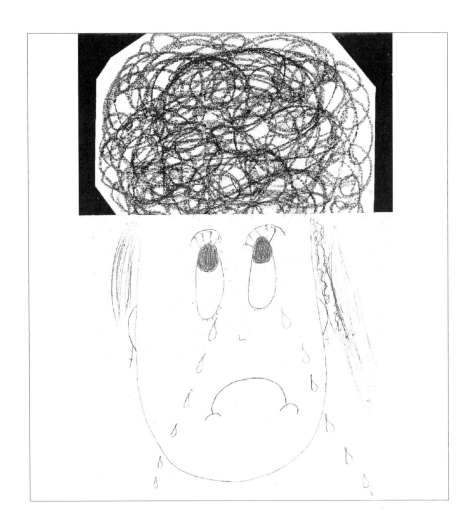

CHAPTER 4

FIGURE 4-9 **Structure:** This two-section drawing is executed in two different media. The top half is drawn in oil pastel and is a complex multicolored configuration of lines. The lower half is a face, simply drawn in pencil. Both parts of the picture show movement. Expressionism is characterized by exaggeration of features in the face, color, and movement in the upper section. The top of the head extends off the top of the page. The upper section of the drawing is drawn on a separate piece of paper that is cut into a crude semi-circle and taped onto the back of the other piece.

Meaning: A cartoon-like countenance depicts a crying girl, her disembodied head floating off the page. She is wearing earrings and her hair is roughly suggested. Her gigantic eyes stare upward at the colored mass emerging from her head. Is this the confusion of a depressed adolescent? Possibly. One distinction seen in this image is that the colorful scribble is not a "cloud" of confusion floating over her; rather, it bursts forth from her forehead, literally separated by placement on a second sheet of paper. In this drawing by an 18-year-old woman with DID, the phenomenon of the "exploding head" is illustrated and concretized by the use of different media and sheets of paper. The position of the eyes is reminiscent of the classic eyeroll technique used to screen the highly hypnotizable trauma victim (Spiegel & Spiegel, 1978).

FIGURE 4-10

Structure: A figure whose torso, limbs, and hair are composed of black zig-zagging lines is the central focus of this picture. Drawn in marker, the figure has no mouth. Irregular lines surrounding this image create a dynamic effect.

Meaning: The electrified quality of this picture portrays tension in the body. This rudimentary configuration by an adult woman, with its visual emphasis on the head, might imply a manic psychosis. Drawn by a child alter of a woman with MPD, it captures the extreme energy and anxiety generated when the personality system is in conflict.

Conclusion The cataclysmic nature of chaos pictures almost requires that expressionism be employed in their creation. In fact, in our experience, no other style was used to make chaos pictures. This means that when movement, distortion, exaggeration, and polychrome are all present in a drawing that in some way seems to illustrate the externalization of conflict, one should consider the possibility of its being a chaos picture. Movement facilitates the depiction of upheaval, interaction, and forceful release. Distortion and exaggeration help give a picture its affective edge by manipulating form—in this case, to convey distress. Likewise, color—usually lots of it—adds to the affective impact of the image. Further, randomness and complexity add to the confusion, disorder, and clutter in the composition. For these reasons, the level of meaning is typically clear in these pictures, since their chaotic nature is quite evident. What remains ambiguous is the origin of the chaos. If the client is not known to have DID, the more subtle implications of the picture (the dynamics within the artist's internal system) might be lost. When the noise, pressure, and physical pain of chaos are no longer tolerable, the ensuing psychic explosion might result in the phenomenon of fragmentation—a different kind of decompensation in which the dissociative process is at its height.

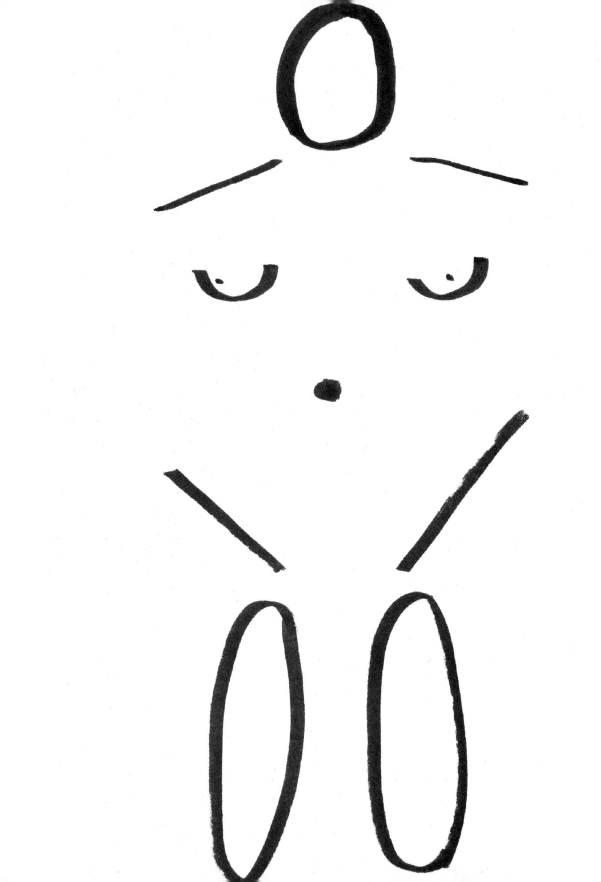

Chapter 5

Fragmentation Pictures
The Fractured Sense of Self

At one time or another, all of us have had the experience of feeling like we were "falling apart." Although it may mean different things to different people, "going to pieces" is a process that is described universally in stories and song, due to its profound impact on the sense of self. Inability to "get oneself together" and regain control of thought, feeling, and action threatens the very core of one's autonomy. For the traumatized person, being "all broken up" about one's life is more than just a figure of speech. According to Spiegel (1991), trauma induces discontinuity in its victims at a variety of levels. The object of interpersonal violence requires escape from the physical and emotional assault; in fact, this is the origin of dissociation during child abuse trauma. The more frequent and intense the discontinuity, the more disjointed one's experience, resulting in intrapsychic chaos. The "not me" of alter personalities' formation and "not now" of time distortion resulting from amnesia reify levels of separateness within the person who dissociates at a pathological rate (Cohen, in press). Additionally, chaos builds in the mind during psychotherapy as secrets are broached, multiplicity is uncovered, and allegiance to perpetrators is scrutinized; this is when the need for disengagement heightens. Depersonalization and numbing have been described as self-regulating anesthesia for the overload of affects associated with trauma (Nathanson, 1992).

Fragmentation of self is a subject that has frequently been written about but little understood (Braude, 1992). Theoretical discussions regarding multiplicity and unity typically focus on the chicken-and-egg origins of the self: Are we born whole only to shatter (like Humpty Dumpty) from early trauma, or do we come into this world as a bundle of states of consciousness that weave together over time into a coherent identity? To further confound this matter, post-modernists have idealized the multiple self in their discourse regarding subjectivity and the influences of gender, class, and race on the perception of external reality (Glass, 1993).

Those who suffer from severe post-traumatic dissociation are frequently eloquent in their descriptions of this state; they talk about psychological as well as physical manifestations of disunity. At one end of the spectrum of fragmentation experiences the "right hand doesn't know what the left hand is doing." During these episodes, executive control may be divided even within the same person (Hilgard, 1977). At the other end, the emotional disarray is so extreme that psycho-physical numbing is induced (much like a breaker switch in an electrical system) and conscious control is lost with regard to volitional speech and action. During these episodes, one is likely to observe robotic behavior in some clients along with severe amnesia.

Fragmentation and its effects can also be a result of the overwhelming feelings that arise during the processing of abuse memories and the conflicts that follow. Putnam (1989, p. 63) has described a "revolving door crisis" in which the person with DID is unable to maintain any stability in a single state of consciousness; hence identity is disjointed.

Fragmentation images that recur in the artwork of people diagnosed with dissociative identity disorder typically include fractured surfaces, shattered remnants, and disembodied limbs. The puzzle metaphor is frequently invoked in written and drawn descriptions.

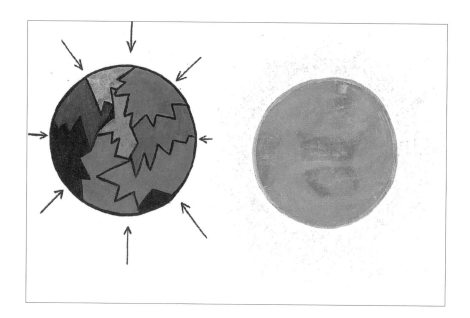

FIGURE 5-1

Structure: Two circles, equal in size, are juxtaposed on a blank page. The circle on the right is edged in gold; its center, diffuse, flowing paint in blue, green, and white. The circle on the left is edged in black; it is composed of jagged interlocking shapes, each a different solid color. Around the outside of the circle are arrows pointed toward it, suggesting movement inward. The circle on the right is similarly surrounded, but by a diffuse haze of glittery speckles, suggesting movement outward. Elementalism is the style of this multimedia picture.

Meaning: These side-by-side images are easily compared. The one on the right depicts wholeness and softness, with a glowing aura, while its counterpart boldly presents its fractured facade under attack from outside (Mills & Cohen, 1993). The juxtaposition of these two gestalts draws the viewer's attention to the artist's sense of brokenness. This is an image that might very well be drawn by anyone feeling the impact of external pressures. The woman with DID who made this particular drawing titled it "World's Apart," a double-edged message about her inner world falling apart as well as the vast difference between these two states of being.

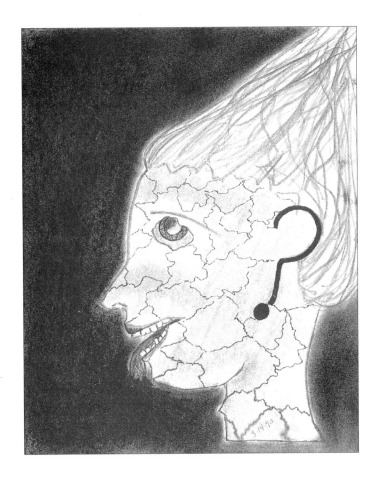

FIGURE 5-2   **Structure:** The profile of a woman is drawn in chalk pastel and marker. Boldly set against a background of black, peach-colored skin is contrasted with a purple ear, a red eye, and grey and yellow hair pulled upward to the right corner of the page. The mouth is open, exposing teeth as well as a tiny hanging figure. The neck ends abruptly with a straight edge; a solid purple circle sits below the ear. The skin is marked by a web of jagged irregular shapes delicately drawn across its surface. **Meaning:** This grotesque portrait incorporates such a number of unconventional, jarring features that one might describe it as bizarre. The presence of the tiny figure hanging from the mouth of the subject reinforces this notion. The fractured surface of the woman's face suggests she is "cracking up" literally and figuratively. Her purple ear and earring form a large question mark, as if to wonder what it all means. When drawn by an individual with a trauma history, a picture of "cracking up" takes on a new dimension. Feelings of fragmentation can wax and wane; when intense, they may compromise the client's level of functioning in her daily life.

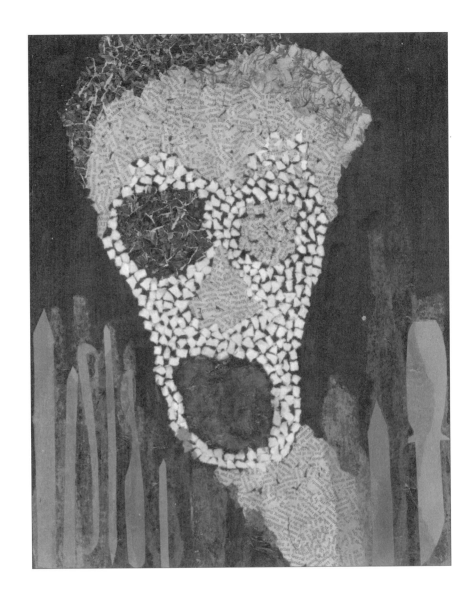

FIGURE 5-3

Structure: Boldly set against a black painted background, tiny bits of news-paper, white paper, red tissue paper, and a magazine photo are pieced together into the image of a distorted face. The circular mouth, filled with transparent red, echoes in color the patterned verticals that flank the image in the lower half of the page. Color, form, and implied movement combine to create a highly expressionistic picture.

Meaning: Reminiscent of Edvard Munch's familiar icon, The Scream, the misshapen head with its open mouth seems about to explode, scattering its hundreds of fragments into the darkness. The visual tension between each glued piece of paper and among the various types of collage materials is heightened by the black, white, and red color. The knives and surgical instruments along the bottom of the page form a frightening fence consumed by red and orange tissue paper flames. The newsprint pieces literally fill the top of the head with words. The style of execution makes this picture more disturbing than most fragmentation pictures. Appreciating the compulsivity of application—tiny scraps affixed one by one—helps the viewer to better understand the artist's temperament, which might be a fruitful avenue for therapeutic investigation. The multiplicity of parts combined with the intensity of the image bespeaks fragmentation. This serves to reframe the ostensibly compulsive nature of the image, while decreasing the ambiguity of the picture's meaning.

FIGURE 5-4

Structure: In the center of this composition are two overlapping, naturalistically painted faces. Surrounding the faces are small angular shapes, painted in blue and grey. Just below the faces is a red rose, its thorns and petals meticulously painted. To the left of these images is the large red profile of a woman's face, its deep blue eye and paper-white skin contrasted against a hot pink background. Movement is implied by the many tiny wedge shapes in this picture; they seem to emanate from the double portrait in the picture's center.

Meaning: Several contrasting elements are featured in this watercolor painting: the hot color of the profile and background are set against the cool colors of the shard-like shapes and the starkness of the white page; the naturalism of the central faces is juxtaposed against the flatness of the red profile; the sharpness of the wedge shapes and thorns counters the smoothness of the rose and the small floating faces. Further, these elements serve to convey a sense of fragility about the maker. The angular fragments seem to be shattered like glass, and the drooping leaves of the rose suggest decay. "We Are Me" is the picture's title, written in the lower right corner of the page. Together the explosion suggested within the head (as in chaos pictures) and the sense of breaking into pieces (typically seen in fragmentation pictures) leave little doubt of multiplicity.

FIGURE 5-5

Structure: White paper shapes are scissor-cut and glued to a background of black construction paper, the edges of which are rough and hand torn. Black marker is used to draw details of the human figure, while red tempera paint marks various points where shapes are disconnected. Wavy red lines circumscribe the lower half of the body. Above the figure, painted in red, is the phrase "PISSED OFF." Movement is indicated by the downward moving red below the head, as well as the dotted marks below the eyes. The distortion of form, bold contrast in color, movement, and overstated theme all contribute to the visual statement of this expressionistic collage.

Meaning: Anger is clearly the theme of this picture, and it is titled as such. The dismembered figure screams, its mouth agape; tears flow from its wide-eyed stare. One might perceive this to be a homicidal or suicidal communication, its victim cut to pieces. But this is hardly a dead body; rather it is hurt, both physically and emotionally. Overwhelming affect frequently results in the experience of disunity in highly dissociative persons. In this instance, one might conjecture that the feeling of anger is so psychologically disruptive to the artist that she "falls apart" in response. The flowing blood concretizes the pain for others to see.

FIGURE 5-6

Structure: In this expressionistic painting, the torso of a human figure is separated from its lower half. Two feet and one hand protrude into the space from the page's edges. Each body part is clearly labeled. Brown, black, and yellow are painted against a background of blue. The composition is characterized by a distortion of the anatomy as well as the random placement of elements.

Meaning: The straightforward labeling of this picture leaves little ambiguity about its basic communicative intent. The sections of this body are severed, or at least disconnected, showing a separation of the lower body (hence the genitalia) as well as the hands and feet. Even the mouth seems to slide off the surface of the face. There is a curious color-coding at work here—the lower body and extremities are painted in black. One might perceive this painting as the work of a psychotic person; however, their images usually depict disconnection between the head and shoulders.

Drawn by a male alter of a female DID patient, the disconnectedness within the body may address not only rejection of the opposite gender's anatomy and the sites of sexual transgressions, but the dissociation of the hands and feet as instruments for perpetration, retaliation, or escape.

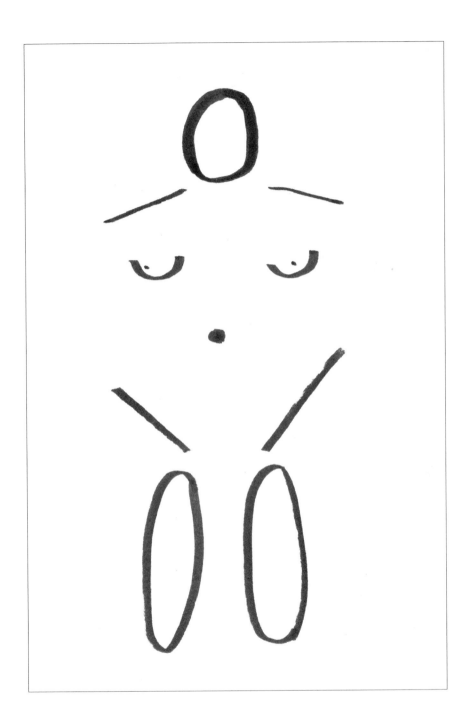

CHAPTER 5

FIGURE 5-7

Structure: An open circle is placed at the top center of the page in this monochromatic marker drawing. The remainder of the image is symmetrical. Below the circle are a pair of short, slanted lines; below the lines are a pair of half circles, open at their tops, a single dot floating within each. In the center of the composition is a single solid dot. Below the dot a pair of lines slant down and inward to a pair of vertical ellipses. There are no colors or embellishments on this bold design.

Meaning: The viewer is reminded of the highly stylized and economical markings on a primitive shield. Most apparent is the disconnected image of a nude woman, suggestive of a client with body-image distortion and depersonalization. Those scrutinizing this image further might also recognize a face organized around the central nose/dot. Bodily disunity in conjunction with double images (such as the face, here) should alert the viewer to the complex internal self-images of people with DID. Though part-selves can command the workings of the body, their behaviors are often disavowed and experienced as nonexistent or accidental. In this drawing, the hidden face watches in a similar manner to hypervigilant alters who attempt to protect the client's physical person from harm. The coded and highly stylized nature of this configuration, with its disconnected limbs, head, and torso, communicates a rather ambiguous message to the viewer.

CHAPTER 5

FIGURE 5-8

Structure: A random composition of body parts pointing upward or to the page's edges is drawn in black marker. Just below the center of the page is a disembodied head above heavily scribbled horizontal lines. The background is the blank page. Movement is indicated in the directionality of the limbs. The careful viewer will count three hands (two with arms) and three legs with feet.

Meaning: Despite the representational approach used in this drawing, few clues are offered to explain the context here; hence the meaning of this image remains obscure. There is nothing overtly gruesome in the presentation of these severed extremities, although the mass below the head might be perceived as blood. As with Figure 5-7, the sense of depersonalization is concretized, which one might also note in the art of schizophrenic patients. The same woman drew this picture who drew Figure 5-7, and her multiplicity provided distinctive contexts for each of the similar-looking drawings. While the former indeed addresses issues of depersonalization, this drawing employs the disconnectedness of repeated body parts as a method for illustrating "stop action" motion. According to the client, the lines beneath the screaming head denote the surface of water in which the figure is drowning; the limbs flail about. In the hypnotic world of the dissociative person, additional details are unnecessary to communicate such an experience. The helplessness of drowning is further reinforced by the disconnections in the body.

FIGURE 5-9

Structure: Various media and methods were used to create this bold composition. White paper is painted over with black tempera with the exception of a vertical rectangular shape at the far right center, near the edge of the page. Inside this shape stands a stick figure in profile. The figure, drawn with marker, extends its arms, palms up. On the upper left of the page three large round shapes of torn white paper are glued down; they have been splattered with red paint. The center and right side circles each have a stick figure drawn in pencil beneath the paint, each with a red mouth. The left side circle contains two concentric circles of tiny stick figures drawn with a pencil. Below the three round shapes, a group of irregularly shaped fragments of torn white paper, also splattered with red paint, reveal elements of drawn stick figures. These pieces are glued against the black background in the configuration of a mound. Juxtaposition is evidenced in the choice of media, application of materials, and imagery.

Meaning: The posture of the figure to the right of the page, as well as its compositional placement, communicates resistance to the images of intense affect suggested by the shapes, colors, and content outside its protective white box. The collaged circles evoke mayhem, their splattered red paint reminiscent of so many violent movies, with victims lying amidst the devastation. The torn paper pieces concretize the process even further; it is not clear, however, what this process represents. Does the act of ripping communicate rejection of the original image, or does it reinforce it?

The chaotic splatter of paint, the hidden array of tiny generic figures, the mutilation of images, and the torn pieces alert the viewer to themes characteristic of the art of individuals with multiple personality. The reader has already been introduced to the graphic phenomenology of the DID system (groups of figures) when it is in chaos (disorganized elements), and can observe here the next step toward psychic disintegration (torn pieces) in the fragmentation picture. In this instance, the drama of ambivalence and powerful urges is externalized against the darkness of the internal environ. Imperceptibly written in black against the black background are the words "choice" and "destiny," indicating the artist's inner struggle regarding self-control of this state.

FIGURE 5-10

Structure: A delicately drawn pen-and-ink rendering of a tree broken near the base of its trunk is the subject of this picture. Moving from the right side of the page to the left, three hollow segments of trunk lie upon the ground (although there is no explicit groundline); one of them is seen in frontal view. The farthest image from the trunk is a large, bare branch. There are no other elements surrounding these fragments. The remainder of the page is blank. The drawing utilizes dimensionality to emphasize the hollowness of the trunk.

Meaning: The simplicity of this image communicates several related themes: death, damage, hurt, emptiness, and isolation. Looking at the pieces of the tree, we can easily visualize it as it once was; but then we are confronted with the reality of its current state eaten away from within and broken. Even the branch resembles a dead creature on its back, limbs in the air. Such affect and content might be seen in the artwork of a depressed person, although the attention to detail implies a high level of energy. One subtle image in this drawing piques the curiosity of the astute observer. The smallest trunk fragment resembles an observing eye. Those who are familiar with the imagery of multiple personality are aware of such disembodied eyes. The fragmentation, eye image, attention to detail, and visual themes identify this as imagery by a severely dissociative client. Hence, the segmentation denotes not simply being broken, but being fragmented and disconnected from its very essence. Additionally, the tree is frequently chosen by individuals with DID as a symbol of self.

Conclusion   Even though MPD clients have to use dissociation to separate psyche and soma, psychological pain and physical distress are nonetheless linked and revealed in their art expressions. While chaos pictures primarily illustrate psychological distress, they also reflect the physiological discomfort experienced by the patient. On the other hand, fragmentation pictures, with their imagery of damaged and disconnected bodies, seem to portray physiological states, but are in fact indicative of the psychological effects of chronic dissociation.

Although any of the four styles can be used effectively to communicate fragmentation, certain artmaking strategies seem to be more commonly employed than others. In contrast to the complexity and clutter of chaos pictures, fragmentation pictures describe a process that is clear and rather direct. Consequently, simplicity and boldness facilitate communication of this experience. Fragmentation has no subsidiary agendas; the message is one of separation, brokenness, and disconnection. Because affect is generally shut off in response to its intensity during this state, color is sparingly used; thus monochrome pictures or those with few colors are more frequently seen. Emphasis here is on compositional and narrative elements.

The spectrum of pictorial fragmentation from fractured to shattered reflects different artmaking strategies. When images retain their original wholeness they may be depicted as simple and bold. Distortion and exaggeration might be used to indicate an altered sense of reality. Those that depict the broken image usually employ randomness to convey the destructive impact of the trauma. The more obviously detached, broken, or severed the image is, the clearer its level of meaning.

The extent of the internal sense of separateness varies according to the severity of the maker's abuse history. The more toxic a memory, for instance, the greater the need may be for maintaining it outside of awareness. Personal information or experiences that require psychological segregation due to their conflictual nature might require the development of amnestic barriers or hallucinatory obstacles to safeguard and restrain the flow of this material.

Chapter 6

Barrier Pictures
Dividing Lines

I n the physical world, space can be delineated two-dimensionally (as in a line drawn on a page) or three dimensionally (as in constructions that extend upward, outward, and downward). The divisions that occur within consciousness of a person with post-traumatic dissociation serve a variety of functions.

Barriers are typically used by people with DID to separate things, places, ideas, part-selves, and feelings. When barriers are used for protection, they can take the form of constructions such as walls and fences or manifest through such phenomena as rainbows, auras, or healing light. Providing passage is another function of barriers; doors and gates allow for transition between places or states of mind. Further, barriers can be used as containers for traumatic images, strong affect, and destructive parts of the self—a purpose that is quite important though, unfortunately, often neglected.

More frequently than not, barriers are used to separate, since the original purpose of dissociative behavior was to leave unpleasant reality for an autohypnotic alternative. Thus, barrier pictures illustrate separations between conscious and dissociated thoughts, feelings and memories, reality and fantasy; between aspects of the inner world; and between the inner and outer worlds.

Hilgard (1977) uses a diagram to show the difference between suppression and amnesia. In it, amnesia is depicted as a vertical barrier, while suppression is depicted as horizontal. It is interesting to note that most barrier pictures studied by the authors divide the picture space vertically rather than horizontally.

Barriers drawn by people with dissociative identity disorder can be as simple as a scratched line on a piece of paper or as elaborate as the finest architectural rendering. When barriers are used for containment and protection, almost any shape goes: seashells, jars, castles, circles, trunks, or moats. The nature of the barrier is usually dictated by the physical requirements of the task. Barriers or passageways may be depicted as graciously open and inviting or defensively barricaded and barred, chained, locked, and nailed shut.

Clearly, barriers serve purposes that are both healthy and pathological; as a childhood survival technique, divided consciousness is quite effective. In adulthood, however, to divide is to self-conquer. Since there are so many ways that barriers can be used in art by people with DID, it is especially important to notice these images and carefully consider their function.

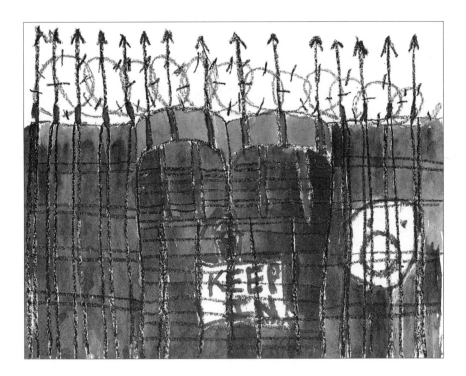

FIGURE 6-1a

Structure: Vertical and horizontal lines drawn in oil pastel create a grid pattern across the full surface of the page. Black is painted in watercolor over the linear elements, creating a single massive shape. Several images are drawn in red: the words "keep in" written within a square, a circular face floating on the right side of the page, and a series of lines above an oval shape. Across the top section of the picture, a row of upward-aiming arrows is superimposed on brown looping lines, punctuated by short strokes, in this bold, expressionist picture.

Meaning: The facade of a castle is suggested, with elaborate protective fencing and a padlocked drawbridge. The red and black combination communicates intense feeling. Although the mouth on the face is wide open, the message on the sign is clear. It warns of the danger of telling secrets; the fortress is depicted as both repository and potential punishment. Were this image drawn by an adolescent protecting his privacy, the sign might more typically read "keep out." For the traumatized dissociative patient, the ability to hold information back is more highly valued, as it ensures safety from internal or interpersonal reprisal. An extraordinary amount of energy is expended in achieving this lifelong goal. The grid-like pattern on the surface of the picture serves to reinforce the barrier between the artist and the viewer.

FIGURE 6-1b Even such a seemingly personal image as the one in Figure 6-1a appeared again in the work of a woman twenty-five years younger. Figure 6-1b was brought to the authors' attention by a graduate student who was working with the young client who drew this picture. During the client's first psychiatric hospitalization, having just received the diagnosis of MPD years and miles apart from the woman who made Figure 6-1a, she drew a virtually identical image. The written message, "keep in," the sharply pointed fenceposts, and the screaming disembodied head (drawn here in white in the lower right corner) figure prominently in both drawings, as do the predominance of black and red.

FIGURE 6-2

Structure: Two simple images are separated by a vertical black line. Boldly painted in purple, pink, orange, and yellow, a flower stands atop a mound of green. The three purple petals form points in a visual triangle. On the right side of the page red and black are swirled together, forming a rectangular mass.

Meaning: The side-by-side placement of these images invites comparison by the viewer. The flower on the left is controlled and organized, while the shape on the right is seething with affect. Separated by a line of demarcation, the dichotomy of these otherwise unrelated configurations is accentuated. Persons with DID use this artmaking strategy to communicate disparities between various aspects of their personal worlds. In this example, the flower depicts a system in harmony, while the expressive abstraction provides a chaotic counterpoint. The colors in the flower petals create an anthropomorphic gestalt in which purple delineates the head and legs, with pink defining the arm; seen in this way, the flower stem impales the figure and its torso appears wounded. Unless one's awareness of the prevalence of barrier pictures in the dissociative population is heightened, productions such as this one remain completely coded and obscure.

CHAPTER 6

FIGURE 6-3

Structure: Chalk pastel and watercolor are paired to create this picture, which is divided down the center by a long vertical squiggle made of one violet and two black lines. On the right is a house, its two square windows glazed in violet. The area surrounding the house is done in yellow pastel, as is the sun in the upper right corner. The tree on the right and the house are drawn in shades of green. Alongside the central dividing line is a column of rectangular shapes that connects to three rows of squarish shapes. A pair of arms extend from the right corner into the space in front of the house.

To the left of the central axis a distorted version of this scene is depicted. The house is painted black, its size smaller than the other and its outlines irregular. The tree is also darker, its foliage emphasized by strokes of paint. The environment around the house is pink. An amorphous shape to the left of the building is painted in black. An armless figure lies at the foot of the walkway, a black configuration resembling a noose attached to its neck. A large black "X" hovers just above the supine figure. A pair of eyes float disembodied next to a single arm in the space in front of the house. A mixture of surrealism and expressionism are used on the left side of the page, while naturalism with a single surreal element is featured on the right, creating a strong juxtaposition.

Meaning: The side-by-side depiction of houses provides a natural opportunity for comparison between the two. Although the one on the right is represented as stereotypical and bright, the disembodied arms add a startling note to the composition. The image on the left is dark, shriveled, and disjointed, owing to the array of body parts strewn around the yard. Clearly the demarcation between the dark and the bright is a very important aspect of this picture, in that there are two dividers separating these two sections of the picture, an abstract shape and a brick wall. On first evaluation one might consider this the work of a psychotic person; it is bizarre and distorted. The double barrier, however, plays a key role in linking this to the productions of individuals with DID. Oftentimes, art therapists use the inside/outside split as a theme in structured art therapy groups. In this case, the patient spontaneously depicted the disparity between the outward appearance of self, home, or family with the distinctly subjective perception of same.

FIGURE 6-4a

Structure: The composition of this picture, meticulously drawn in pencil, is comprised of two segments separated by a vertical element, which has a curvilinear motif along its length. On the right side of the page is a seated figure atop a stool; her ankle is chained to a large black ball. Behind her is a curtain. On the left side of the picture are six small figures grouped in a somewhat sequential pattern around a central figure whose arms are open at his sides. Although the scenario is depicted in a naturalistic style, with an emphasis on dimensionality, there are no identifying environmental elements. **Meaning:** Despite the specifically delineated narrative in this picture, its exact nature is somewhat ambiguous. Is one looking at a fairy tale? Is this a self-representation of the artist? One is immediately struck by the wizened female figure, isolated by a permeable wall (the curtain) as well as an abstract one (the decorative pattern). Each of the young figures on the left seems to be carrying something; what is their relationship to the seated figure? Since there are obsessive and depressive qualities to this drawing (mostly related to its execution), one might wonder whether an anorexic client drew it. However, an anorexic client would be unlikely to show so much awareness of her own body-image. The repeated barrier and the grouping of children are clues to potential dissociation and multiplicity.

FIGURE 6-4b

Drawn by the client after a week of intensive inpatient treatment, this picture further illustrates the internal saga. The figures on the left have gathered to bring sustenance, light, and comforts to the starving girl chained behind the "Wizard of Oz" curtain. In the sequel drawing, the chained girl is safely asleep, guarded by a protector, surrounded by gifts of food and light. Even the space she is given on the page is broadened. As described by the woman diagnosed with DID who drew these images, the alter personalities on the left are joined in collaboration; they are watched over by the winged figure. In this transformation, the decorative barrier has narrowed. The use of monochromatic pencil and meticulous attention to detail in this pair of pictures reinforce the sense of emotional detachment.

CHAPTER 6

FIGURE 6-5 **Structure:** A vertical wall separates two female figures. At one end of a rope is a young girl standing on her toes; at the other end, a woman grips the rope and hangs just below the top of the wall. Simply drawn in pen and ink, movement is suggested by the tension in the rope, its slack end laying on the floor beside the girl.

Meaning: A little girl seems to be pulling a grown woman over the top of a high wall. There is relative ease in the posture of the girl and the length of the rope at her feet, juxtaposed with the strained posture of the woman, literally at the end of her rope. Might this struggle be a tug-of-war between a child and her mother? One wonders at the unexpected power of the youngster.

Surmounting an obstacle seems to be one message of this picture; opposition of figures on either side of a barrier might be another. There is little reason to expect multiplicity from an image such as this; however, since this artist is diagnosed with DID, the barrier between present and past and between part-selves is evident. Once an accurate diagnosis has been made, the message of this highly ambiguous image is clarified. In the course of DID therapy, the adult consciousness (right side of page) must surmount the barrier to get to the repressed or dissociated unconscious (left side of page) childhood material.

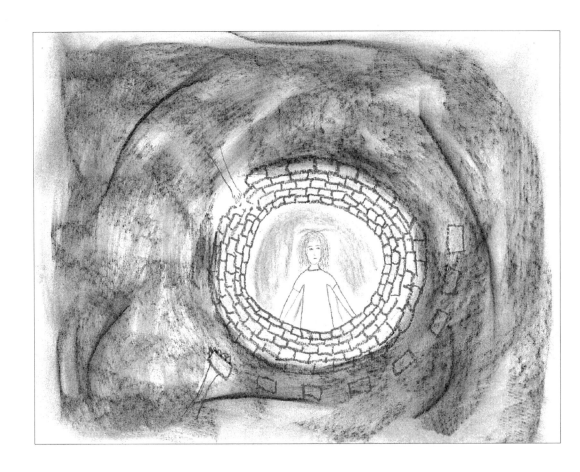

CHAPTER 6

FIGURE 6-6

Structure: A young female figure in white is enclosed within a ring of multi-layered red rectangles. The figure is surrounded by pale blue, while the ring is surrounded by smeared black chalk pastel. Disembodied arms reach out from the dark area for the red rectangles. A patch of white surrounds the hand in the upper part of the picture. A series of red rectangles are also sequentially placed in the lower part of the page. The figure is drawn in pencil, while the rectangles are drawn in oil pastel.

Meaning: The juxtaposition of dark and light, inner and outer, and open and closed provides the thematic thrust of this disorienting image. The lack of logical orientation to up/down and inside/outside creates a surreal quality. A brick wall separates the figure from the dark foreboding haze surrounding it. Depression and isolation are suggested here. The hands both place and remove bricks from the wall; this image begs further investigation. The young alter personality, depicted in the purity of her white garb, is being protected as well as segregated within the artist's personality system. The compartmentalization of information held by this particular part-self is achieved by the construction of the amnestic barrier. Another personality is attempting to open communication.

FIGURE 6-7 **Structure:** A vaguely articulated black shape is placed at the bottom center of the page. Above it is a plane of beige; irregular black lines emanate from a central point on this plane from which marks of blue move downward. A dab of red is at the center of this configuration of lines, which is the visual focal point of this chalk pastel drawing. Movement and dimensionality can be seen in the gradation of dark and light curving blue shapes in the top half of the picture. A second plane of beige is located at the top of the page, above the blue area.

Meaning: A cracking wall is the central image of this expressionistic drawing; it mediates between the diminutive figure and the vast expanse of water moving toward the wall. Flooding is a metaphor for feeling overwhelmed; the dam is clearly about to burst. This is an understandable response to being immersed in therapy. The presence of the barrier, holding back massive energy, is a clue for the observer searching for dissociative imagery. Flooding, a term frequently used to describe the experience of individuals with severe post-traumatic stress disorder, refers to the patient's inability to modulate affect. In the case of DID, dissociative barriers hold back unacceptable thoughts, feelings, or memories. The alter personality of this client, whose traumatic memories may break through her dissociative defenses at any moment, seems especially vulnerable due to its size, shape, and posture. The bright red spot at the center of the crack further reflects the pain of this experience. Therapists treating DID clients who create such images would do well to lower the intensity of treatment and allow the defenses to work on behalf of the system, rather than against it.

FIGURE 6-8

Structure: A young girl presses against a door. Drawn in monochrome fine tip marker, the image depicts a cutaway view in which large biomorphic shapes fill the space behind the door; dimensionality is thus suggested. Juxtaposition is used to create a surreal situation.

Meaning: Although the viewer may not know exactly what the material behind the door represents, the girl is clearly defending against its intrusion into her environment (which is quite bare). Certainly, this is not a picture drawn by a child; it is the work of an adult. It overtly communicates active suppression of an overwhelming, expanding substance, but denies the viewer further clues to its meaning. This burgeoning growth most likely represents something traumatic bursting from behind a barrier. The artist recently spoke of this picture, saying, "I had forgotten what those shapes said in that picture; did you see the word behind the door? It says 'future'." For some, the notion of future is fraught with unspeakable anxiety and fear. The authors, in fact, had not seen the word in the shapes behind the door (once seen, however, it becomes unavoidable). This illustrates the effectiveness of coding; even using words, messages can be disguised.

FIGURE 6-9   **Structure:** Tempera paint is used in this multicolored expressionist work. Overlapping hands face opposite directions; the hand at the center of the page is beside a vertical divider, which is painted in blue and yellow. To the left of the vertical is a rectangle of loosely painted black. Color is used to effect high contrast, and relative flatness of form contributes to boldness of design. The hands are juxtaposed to one another and, compositionally, to the rectangle of black on the opposite side of the page. Red paint near the fingers suggests downward movement. Differences in color create patterning in the hand images both through the segmentation of the fingers and the separation of groups of fingers.

Meaning: The combination of boldness, color, and style communicates intense affect. Movement and color suggest dripping blood, which tells a narrative of fingers scraping against a barrier. The dripping blood represents both the difficulty of the activity and the resulting pain. The black on the other side of the barrier is dark and unarticulated, which further extends the theme: pursuit of the unknown. Anyone in the midst of therapy might identify with this situation. For the client with DID, the quest for knowledge is typified by the breaking of amnestic barriers to gain access to traumatic memories. The opposing position of the hands may indicate the ongoing struggle about revealing secrets, further underscored by the concretized pain. The meaning of the painting is ambiguous.

FIGURE 6-10

Structure: Chalk pastel is used to draw a symmetrical composition bisected by an irregular vertical red line. In the upper right corner is a circular yellow form interspersed with blue. In the upper left corner is a similar configuration drawn in black, red, and blue. These colors are also seen in the large biomorphic shape on the right side of the page. Opposite, on the left side, a kneeling figure holds a shield in one hand and sword in another. This figure is cut from a magazine. Layered wavy lines of greens and black run across the bottom of the page; two biomorphic configurations are placed in each lower corner. Pale blue is scumbled across the background. Movement is suggested by the wavy line quality throughout the picture, which, combined with saturated polychrome and distortion of form, characterizes expressionism.

Meaning: The central focus in this picture is the thrusting action of the young protagonist with the sword. The target of his attack is a distorted, upright figure on two legs, which also seems to hold a weapon. Color combinations of black, blue, and red suggest bruising, and the biomorphic shapes resemble wounds. The two suns draw attention to the theme of duality in this picture. The young hero depicted here fighting against an apparently dark force of some sort is rather archetypal; since this was drawn by a woman in her forties, however, one wonders at the maker's identification with the adolescent male character. These various clues might lead the viewer to begin wondering about the possibility of DID in this client. The woman who made this picture explained that it illustrated a male alter personality battling with an internal embodiment of her abuse. The dark and light reflect the polarity engendered by this internal conflict.

FIGURE 6-11 **Structure:** Charcoal pencil was used to render this naturalistic landscape of a broken barbed wire fence. The fence posts are arranged sequentially across the page. Two birds fly overhead. Grass grows in the foreground; nothing is depicted in the space beyond the fence.

Meaning: There are few cues in this simple image to catch the attention of even the trained observer of art productions. Barbed wire connotes a specific kind of fence, designed to keep certain things in and certain things out by caus-ing harm or pain to the transgressor. In this image, the wires are down or broken, allowing easy movement from one side to the other. The flying birds are juxtaposed both compositionally and conceptually. They have freedom of movement regardless of the status of the barrier. Largely unremarkable for a drawing by a psychiatric patient, the theme of freedom versus restraint is the only evident level of meaning.

With the benefit of hindsight, one can look again at this drawing, which was made before a diagnosis of DID was given to this artist. The dangerous barrier, meant to restrain memories and personalities from consciousness, is bro-ken through on the left of the page. The fence wire on the right remains intact. Using the past/present orientation to page space as an interpretive device, one might consider the defenses in present consciousness as strong, despite the collapsing of unconscious barriers. The fence posts may mark passages of time along a continuum. The birds may represent aspects or personalities that are free to traverse the inner and outer worlds. It is important to note that the artist offers no information about what lies beyond. There is ambiguity in this communication despite knowledge of the artist's diagnosis.

FIGURE 6-12s The four mixed media pictures reproduced in Figure 6-12s are chosen from an extensive series created by one woman; they chronicle her breakthrough of a post-traumatic amnestic barrier. These particular examples are early in the series' chronology. In the first picture, a purple trapezoid shape—the impassable wall—stands in the darkness, surrounded by black. An adult hand guides a child's; together they hold a pair of keys, as if to unlock the secrets beyond the wall, while a youngster peers out from behind.

Emphasis is placed on the visual weight of the purple wall in the second drawing, as the young girl strains to hold it up. In the small break at the center of the wall is a hand. Blood flows from the wall's lower corner. The affective tone in the next picture is different: the colors brighten, positive phrases are collaged onto the page; where there was blood there is now a teddy bear. The fourth picture draws our attention to the enlarged break in the wall with the little girl seated facing it. The complexity of the background colors in the previous pictures gives way to the movement of birds' flight. The pointing hand is placed adjacent to the warning "proceed with caution."

Using the integrative method to study this group of pictures more closely, we see that boldness, exaggeration, juxtaposition, and movement are used to create an expressionist-surrealist narrative. By attending to the transformation of each image across the series, one can follow the changes as they occur in the client's internal world. The keys, hands, wall, opening, girl, etc., can be used to further enhance imagery work or hypnosis in therapy.

Conclusion

It is not surprising that barrier pictures, after system pictures, are the most frequently seen category in the art of people with DID. This is because dividedness is the essence of the dissociated mind; massive amounts of psychic energy are expended on separating, allocating, and compartmentalizing images, information, and feelings. The page is perfect for externalizing this process, since any linear mark placed upon it dissects its surface.

Protection is attempted by keeping some things in while keeping others out. Part-selves and traumatic memories are isolated one from another in hopes of achieving clarity of thought amidst burgeoning chaos. Overwhelming stimulation and affect are thus diminished. Additionally, a careful distinction between the inner world and consensual reality is effectively maintained by establishing these self-preserving (yet ultimately self-defeating) boundaries.

Barrier pictures are drawn in all art styles, but two are more frequently seen: naturalism and expressionism. Naturalism most easily conveys the narrative aspect of these communications, which, consciously intended or not, are descriptive of the lifelong defensive distribution of consciousness. Vertical markings expeditiously signify walls or doors. A simple horizontal line that breaks and then continues can be "read" as an entryway or exit. Little skill is required to further develop these elements into depictions of architectural realities.

Highlighting the juxtaposition of elements—virtually the hallmark of all barrier pictures—in a pronounced, bisected context conveys a message that something feels fundamentally divided within. An informed viewer who notices barrier pictures drawn repeatedly over a period of time should begin to follow the ambiguous clues, which may eventually lead to diagnosing dissociative identity disorder.

When the picture's story concerns breaking through the barricade, movement is usually introduced; these barrier pictures are typically created in an expressionist style. Change and transformation are the central focus here. Distortion of form is often used to distinguish subjective from objective realities. Interrelationship of images is the primary strategy employed to communicate the correspondance between separated elements, and symmetry is more likely found here than in any of the other categories. Many of these pictures feature boldness and simplicity, which give them a quality of directness when there is a need to communicate a sense of dividedness and urgency related to breaking through the barrier. Dimensionality is sometimes used to concretize the metaphor of the barrier. Unfortunately for most DID clients, lying on the other side of these barriers are other intimidating and potentially dangerous part-selves.

Chapter 7

Threat Pictures
Danger from Within

I n addition to the many stresses and potential threats of the
contemporary world, the severely traumatized, dissociative adult must
also struggle with inner dangers. In the majority of MPD systems certain
alter personalities perpetuate the threat of abuse. Even more frightening,
these threats are often acted upon in various ways, with outcomes ranging
from annoyance to annihilation.

Self-harm in its many forms, including cutting, burning, head banging,
hair pulling, ingestion of toxic and caustic substances, and insertion of foreign
objects into the body are among the more alarming behavioral manifestations
of threat. Strategic dissociative amnesia, oppositional attitudes, and the
outright unavailability of the client are some of its psychological indicators. At
times, one part-self is out to destroy another part, resulting in the outward
appearance of suicidality.

Beahrs (1982), Putnam (1989), and Ross (1989) have described the
phenomenology of the curious and vexing dilemma of self-injury. They
propose a variety of etiological theories, including the externalization of a
good-evil split, transformation of hurt and rejected child parts, and internaliza-
tion of actual persecutors. Although their treatment approaches vary
according to the hypothesized origin of destructive parts, virtually all agree
that one must understand and negotiate with these ostensibly villainous alters
if treatment is to be successful.

Several key issues in the dynamics of the person with DID are played out
in self-threatening behavior. For instance, the reveal-conceal conflict is

107   THREAT PICTURES

concretized through the creation of an alter whose raison d'etre is terrorization of the client and enforcement of the abuser's "don't tell" rule. Additionally, ongoing reenactment of trauma is given a compelling and readily available arena (Chu, 1991; van der Kolk, 1987).

Threat drawings, which illustrate this phenomenon, can, like behavioral indicators, be misunderstood. Paradoxically, they are usually seen as other-directed, even by informed therapists (Coons, 1988); the patient's inner-outer and self-other disorientation thus contaminates the clarity of the communication.

The verbal threat internalized by the severely traumatized child is frequently expressed in the creative productions of the adult survivor. Consequently, threat pictures are more likely than others in the ten categories to contain writing. They are created in a variety of ways, ranging from highly concrete to cryptically symbolic. Images that are often found in threat pictures include blood, staring eyes, weapons of all sorts, arrows focused around central elements, and lightning bolts.

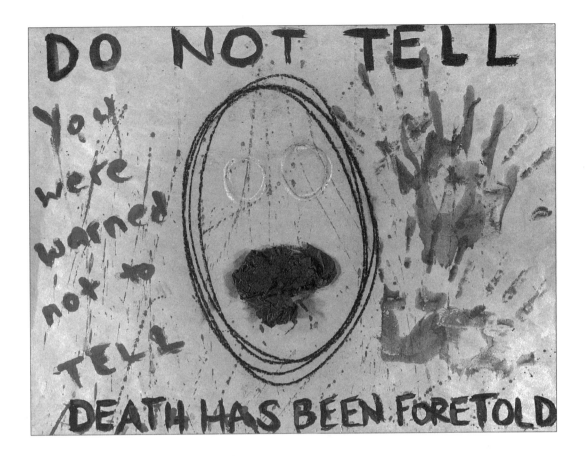

FIGURE 7-1

Structure: Distortion, exaggeration, and movement are combined with boldly painted phrases and placed around the central schema of a face. Like the lettering above and below, the face is drawn in black. Black tissue paper is crumpled and glued into the mouth area, which is painted in red. On the right side of the page appear two sets of handprints, both in red. Additionally, red paint is splattered across the surface of this expressionistic picture. Only the circles of the eyes are drawn in white chalk.

Meaning: "Do Not Tell" blares the message written on this picture; "Death Has Been Foretold." The wadded paper stuffed into the mouth and the use of red paint to denote blood further warn the maker of the punishment to come. Despite these blatant indicators, clinicians unfamiliar with abusers' threats might perceive this powerful image as the frenzied expression of a paranoid person whose secret information is in danger of being exposed. For this reason, even images whose messages are apparently clear may be otherwise perceived by the viewer.

FIGURE 7-2

Structure: Done in colored marker, the drawing is divided into five sections. At the top, a large head is drawn in black with a similarly-sized irregular circle adjacent to it, filled with writing. Below it, a similar head, drawn in red, is connected to a biomorphically shaped form; the two heads overlap slightly. In the lower left corner is a small kneeling figure facing the left edge of the page, with her arms bent at the elbows pointing upward. This figure is drawn in blue and orange. This boldly drawn, expressive image features exaggeration and distortion through the juxtaposition in size between the heads and the figure.

Meaning: Even without reading the lengthy messages inside the word bubbles, the piercing stares, bared teeth, upright hair, use of black and red, and looming faces are threatening in relation to the childlike figure. The invective aimed at the tiny praying figure insinuates a discrepancy between the innocence of what seems to be a young girl and the vehement insults of these accusers. The drawing clearly depicts an abusive relationship; critical parents or perpetrators certainly come to mind. The floating and disembodied heads, which are also transparent where they overlap, alert the viewer to the possibility of introjected entities rather than actual people. Once this option is considered, one can easily recognize the threats of angry alter personalities, which are typically internalized aspects of the abuse.

FIGURE 7-3

Structure: A bold red handprint in tempera paint floats above a vertical broken line drawn in red marker. A written phrase on the right is juxtaposed with this image. Other than the date, there are no extraneous marks on the page. The simplicity of this image is typical of elementalism.

Meaning: This image was made by the client dipping her hand in wet paint and printing it onto the paper, making it look like a bloody handprint. The phrase "death to the woman" suggests a homicidal threat. As a potential target, the viewer (especially if a woman) may feel threatened; indeed, therapists presented with similar drawings have interpreted them as representative of negative feelings towards them. Within the context of DID art production, the viewer and artist are one and the same. As with most DID threat pictures, the next step is to establish whether the conflict that exists is between alters in the battlefield of the patient, which alters in particular are the source of difficulty, and what issues are being acted out.

dead to you

FIGURE 7-4

Structure: A distorted orange arm extends from a mass of yellow lines that extend in every direction from an open shape. The arm is bisected with a black line, scribbled over by red. Red lines criss-cross the hand. Three words are written in lower case just below the container. Distortion and movement are two strategies utilized in this expressionistically drawn picture.

Meaning: A bleeding arm reaches out from a crucible of fire. The words "dead to you" further amplify the message of destruction in this picture. If seen as a suicidal communication from its maker, the message "I am `dead to you'" is relatively clear. Again, the therapist/viewer might wonder about her own safety, until she realizes that the picture is drawn by a patient with diagnosed or suspected DID. The woman who drew this image explained that it depicted the struggle between her alters regarding the need to maintain secrecy. The threat of cutting and burning is explicitly communicated among these part-selves, who refer to each other as "you." To the unsuspecting viewer, the meaning of this drawing might rest with the suicidal aspect of its message, heightened affectively by the expressionistic style, but additional levels of meaning, idiosyncratic to the patient with DID, complicate its message.

FIGURE 7-5

Structure: A large pair of eyes float near the top of this composition. Below them, two knives (one vertical and the other diagonal) are placed into a ground of red at the bottom of the picture. An elongated black shape is placed in the lower right quadrant of the page. Red and black are scumbled across the surface, suggesting movement. Painted in acrylic, the red and black image is punctuated by shiny silver. Five pairs of elliptical shapes superimposed with contrasting color circles are symmetrically placed on the page. The exaggerated size of the eyes, the movement implied by the daubed paint, and the boldness of execution contribute to the expressionist style of this painting.

Meaning: The viewer cannot avoid the intense gaze looking out in terror and surprise. The blood red paint, gun and knives, and suggested movement combine to create a scenario of violent activity. To the right and left of the knife at center are droplets of red over droplets of silver; blood and tears may be signified by these images, as well as by the stippled red that bridges the eyes and the broad area across the bottom of the page. The intermingling of bleeding and crying indicates that this is a victim's message rather than a perpetrator's. One might otherwise wonder about the wide-eyed stare of a paranoid person who might be violent in self-protection. Elsewhere in this book, it has been noted that the ubiquity of black and red, blood as pain, and the presence of staring eyes should raise the level of suspicion concerning dissociative identity disorder. Additional pairs of crying eyes (implied by the images in the upper left and right) strengthen this likelihood.

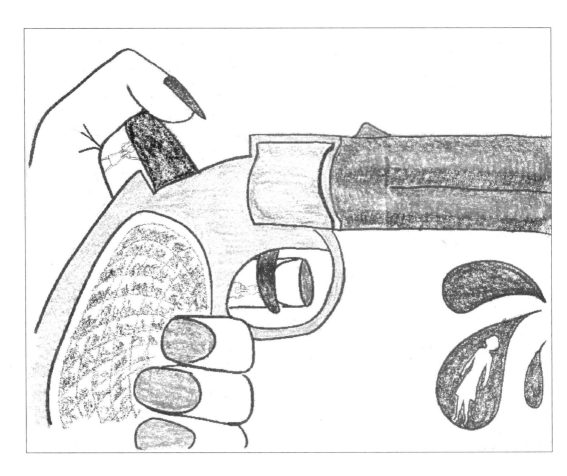

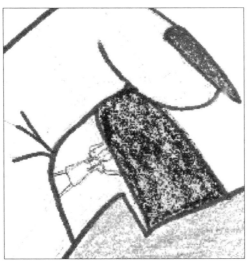

FIGURE 7-6b

FIGURE 7-6a

Structure: A hand cocks the trigger of a pistol in this bold mixed media drawing. Tiny figures of young girls stand with their arms outstretched, impeding movement of the hammer and trigger (see detail, Figure 7-6b). They are exaggerated in their juxtaposition with the hand and gun. Each fingernail on the large hand is a different color, drawn in crayon. Three drops of red emanate from the lower left of the page, suggesting movement. The central one contains the white silhouette of a woman. The handle of the gun is patterned in a checkerboard fashion. The combination of these pictorial elements creates a surreal situation.

Meaning: A gun is about to be shot, but the presence of blood at the right suggests it may not be for the first time. The figure within the large blood drop represents the victim, as well as her pain. Tension is created between the tiny girls and the implied pressure of the large fingers on the hammer and trigger of the gun. Such a picture drawn in therapy may reflect homicidal or suicidal ideation in its maker. The tiny figures may be conceived as symbols of ambivalence regarding the act itself. In any event, the potential lethality is clear.

The juxtaposition of adults and children in this surrealist context should alert one to the possibility of dissociative states in the maker. The internal drama among the various alter personalities in persons with DID is frequently seen in their artwork. Here a patient illustrates her own internal struggle regarding self-harm. The child alters actively fight back against violent urges. In DID, suicidality is a chronic dilemma and often becomes the focus of treatment due to its constant threat. Differently colored fingernails and the patterned gun handle more than likely indicate others in the system of alter personalities. The woman silhouetted in the blood refers to the body of the patient. Since the victim's identity is unknown without the patient's clarification, the ultimate meaning of this picture remains ambiguous.

FIGURE 7-7

Structure: Realistically rendered in black fine tip marker, a blindfolded girl faces front, drawing a bow and arrow. Perspective is indicated by the arrow's foreshortened shaft. The figure is placed in the center of the page. Nothing surrounds her, underscoring the sharp focus and directness of this image. Relatively few lines are used to portray the figure.

Meaning: The artmaking strategies employed in this simply drawn image all support the clarity of its presentation. Not only is the girl drawing her arrow, but she is pointing it directly at the viewer. The fact that she is blindfolded adds an unexpected twist and another dimension to the implications of this action. Alter personalities threaten each other or the patient's body—this is what is portrayed. The blindfold suggests a lack of awareness within the system of this self-persecutory dynamic. The victimized child is acting as the aggressor, her arrow's shaft with rounded head suggesting a penis. The threat embodied in this image is clear, but the identity of its recipient remains ambiguous until a diagnosis of DID is established and conflicts among parts of the internal system explored.

FIGURE 7-8   **Structure:** A hand severed below the wrist reaches from the lower left corner into the central space of the page. Drawn in black ink and embellished with red watercolor, the fingernails are highlighted and visually linked to the red shapes below the hand. Distortion is achieved subtly by the inclusion of two extra fingers. Long carpenters' nails pierce the flesh at more than three points. A band of violet holds together the cleft pieces of the wrist. Boldly executed against a stark white background, this drawing combines elements of naturalism and expressionism for a surrealistic effect.

Meaning: The sadism in this image commands the viewer's attention, while the artmaking strategies employed by the artist heighten the visual impact. The message bespeaks self-mutilation on the most immediate level and therefore may be erroneously assumed to be the work of a client with borderline personality disorder; however, violence is a frequent theme in the threat pictures of people with DID as well. Further, the extra fingers suggest multiplicity.

FIGURE 7-9

Structure: In this line drawing, a young girl holds a mirror whose frame is comprised of two snakes. A pointing hand extends from the center of the mirror. To the right of the hand is an apple, stabbed by a knife, dripping blood. The silhouette of a woman is drawn on the right side of the apple. An eye is juxtaposed with the leaf of the apple. Above the hand is a hanging lightbulb. To the left of the lightbulb is an open mouth with droplets falling into it. This highly surreal composition features a variety of juxtapositions. Exaggeration is used in the silhouette image, which shrinks a human figure to the size of an apple.

Meaning: The central focus of this elaborate and mysterious drawing is the hand pointing at the girl from the mirror. The various images around the hand provide additional information and symbolic context to the meaning of this picture. Decoding these clues, however, is easier said than done. One might think that such illogical and disturbing imagery would be the product of psychosis. This picture, however, has a sense of internal logic and is in fact the epitome of threat from within by an individual with DID.

Juxtaposition of many images weaves an intricate tapestry of meaning. The recipient of the threat is apparent, since she is being targeted by the pointing finger. It is obvious that the threat is from within, since she is looking into a hand mirror. The threat is further amplified by the knife stabbed into the apple. The leaf-eye of the apple watches the girl while literally referring back to the artist, an adult woman, in the form of the silhouette. A snake curled around the girl's wrist is another menacing element. Snakes are rich in symbolic association; nearly every system of symbol interpretation ascribes meaning to them. Although the meaning of the lightbulb and open mouth images is ultimately known only to the artist, they seem to refer to the abuse, about which she is forbidden to speak. The fact that the protagonist holding the mirror is a child in a drawing by an adult is one more indication of multiplicity. The client's inability to explain this picture attests to the obscurity of its meaning, as well as to the potency of its threat.

FIGURE 7-10

Structure: Simple linear images rendered in crayon float around a centrally located solid triangular shape. Tension is created by the juxtaposition of the vertical orientation of the three images on the left side of the page with the horizontals on the right. The image of a knife bridges the two sides across the bottom of the page; two droplets fall from its tip. Movement is also indicated by the spiral at the upper right and the numerous directionals suggested by the various pointed shapes. The entire picture is drawn in monochrome red in the elemental style.

Meaning: The grouping of sharp and pointed objects drawn in red might signify aggression and anger, and the spiral has been cited as an indicator of suicidality in art therapy literature (Wadeson, 1980). This is further reinforced by the knife dripping blood. The structural organization heightens the impact of the color and content in this picture. When drawn by a patient with DID, such imagery typically refers to self-injurious behaviors originated within the personality system. In this example, however, there is no graphic reference to the instigator or recipient of the threat. Although the message of danger is clear, the overall communication remains ambiguous due to the simplicity and emotional detachment at both the structure and content levels.

Conclusion   Juxtaposition is frequently used in threat pictures, both in the pairing of words and images, and in the implied relationship between a weapon and its intended target, which draws attention to impending acts of vengeance. Such drawings include a variety of styles, each of which is organized around a similar compositional strategy; the primary shape or image is impinged upon by one or more external forces.

Expressionism is the style that best communicates the strong feelings inherent in these pictures; intense color, the movement of an attack, and visual overstatement are common. Surrealism can also facilitate the externalization of threats that originate in and are inseparable from the trance logic of the dissociative inner realm. That an abuser can be trapped inside an adult and continue to actually endanger her life requires the suspension of disbelief that accompanies this style.

Once the viewer is sensitized to the visual characteristics of threat pictures, it is difficult to overlook these typically bold creations, which, like warnings, are direct. Additionally, threat pictures often feature the combination of black and red, signifying rage and despair. Exaggeration is used to visually amplify the message of threat. Movement is a strategy that accentuates a dynamic message of impending harm. Although these pictures clearly communicate a strong sense of menace, the true object of their focus is rarely evident. Even in images like Figure 7-7, the viewer may not consider the artist imperiled, especially since the weapon is pictorially pointed outward. However, given the impact of these part-selves' actions on the physical well-being of DID patients, neither the pictures nor their messages should be ignored.

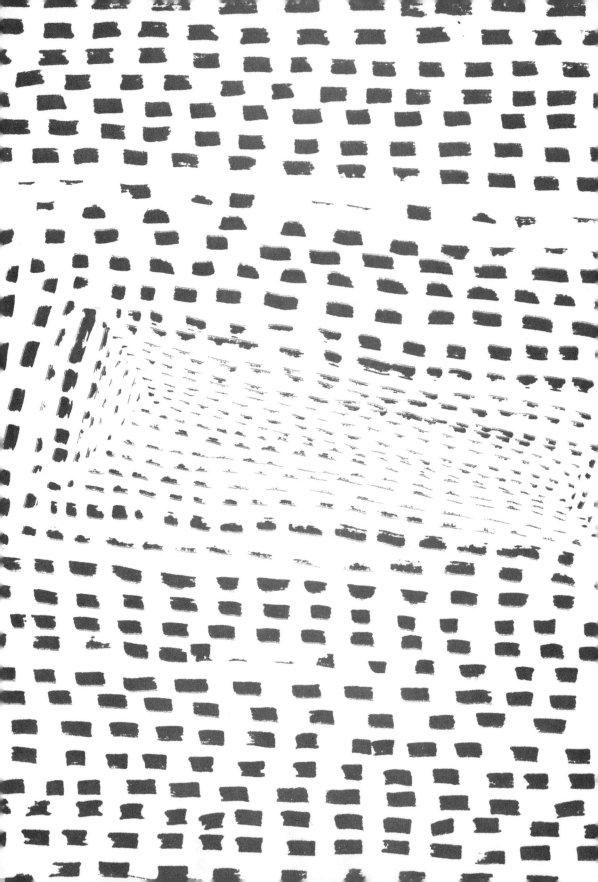

Chapter 8

Induction Pictures
Self-Hypnotic Process

W atching a young child at play, one notices the ease with which he or she slips in and out of different states of consciousness. Imitative activity may alternate with non-directed exploration or even blissfully unfocused reverie. Digging earth, scooping sand, or sloshing water can facilitate the shift to an altered state of consciousness, just as the kinesthetic repetitions that character-ize pounding can free the mind to run on "automatic pilot." In fact, the more physically and emotionally intense an activity, the easier it is to get lost in. Dancing to rock music, for instance, allows for kinesthetic and affective release, while offering an opportunity to "space out" or mentally disconnect.

Physicality is the essential ingredient of induction pictures, which record the self-hypnotic process on paper. This is most evident in the art of highly dissociative children whose pathology results from abuse. Sobol and Cox (1991, 1992) were the first to identify this relationship through research using an art assessment tool called the Child Diagnostic Drawing Series. They noticed the prevalence of certain kinds of marks; these included dots, scribbles, meandering lines, smears, layers, and slashes. Sobol and Cox hypothesized that these drawing behaviors signaled the shifting of states of consciousness through fluid self-soothing rhythms or staccato release of pent-up anxiety.

Others have theorized regarding the significance of these types of marks in the art and imagery of adults. Kellogg (1984), for instance, posited that randomly placed dots graphically reflect dissociative or hypnotic states. Lemozi (cited in Giedion, 1962, p. 151) attributed several meanings to dots, among them "a wound, a personal brand mark . . . a mouth, an eye, the head of a man . . . breasts." Dots, meandering lines, and spirals are frequently found in cave art as well as in the induction pictures of adult dissociative clients. Spirals have been described as figures intended to "induce a state of ecstasy and to enable man to escape from the material world" (Cirlot, 1962, p. 292). Meandering lines, a type of doodling, typically illustrate the unfocused quality of this state, while spiraling or circuitous lines reflect a drifting graphic behavior that can be self-hypnotic or trance-inducing. Doodling, in fact, is a type of graphic play during which the doodler becomes a spectator of the product of his own actions (Van Sommers, 1984), much like the dissociative client. The person with DID who shifts among states of consciousness in order to function or escape can use repetitive actions such as pounding, daubing, or rubbing with art materials to facilitate the necessary transfer of attention.

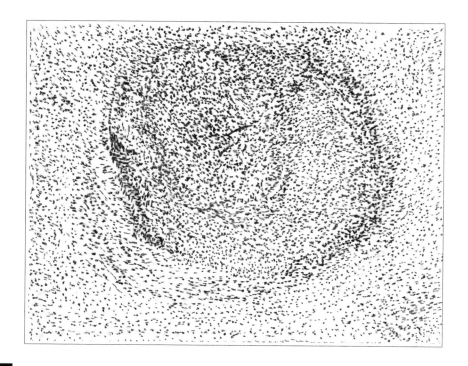

FIGURE 8-1

Structure: Thousands of small green, black, violet, and blue marks cover the page in a random fashion in this marker drawing. Shifts in density of marks add to the complexity of the image; proximity of dots increases at the sides and bottom of the page, creating diffusion. Dynamism occurs around the center of the page, creating a spiraling effect. The flatness of the composition and the overall use of the basic dot markings are typical of the elemental style.

Meaning: The dots are animated in the fashion of a swarm of insects; there is no clear pattern, but the swirling movement implies instability and potential for an infinite variety of changes. A chaotic perseveration and high energy level seem to drive the proliferation of marks. The vague composition, which has no focus, suggests a lack of boundaries. One might view this drawing as the meaningless result of repetitive motor activity, possibly by an individual with chronic schizophrenia or neurological impairment. For the dissociative client, the dotting represents a graphic recording of the psychological diffusion that occurs when shifting into a trance. Meaning in pictures such as this one is quite obscure because it lacks specific compositional clues and recognizable content elements, even for an abstraction.

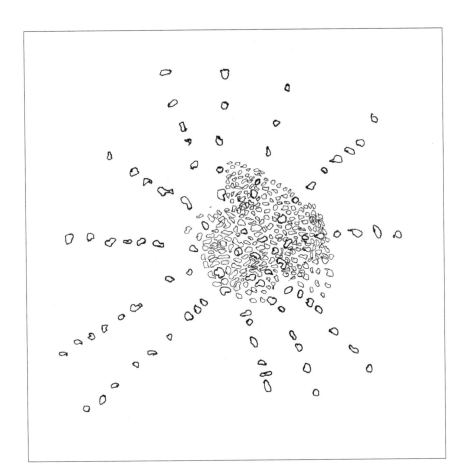

FIGURE 8-2

Structure: This line drawing features a central mass of tiny, black, irregular, circular shapes. Around the perimeter of the central image, similar tiny shapes form sequential arrangements, creating a radial pattern. There are no other colors in this picture, and the remainder of the space is white. Movement is implied by the fragments that radiate from the circular center. Here is an excellent example of elementalism in an abstraction, where the graphic elements are reduced to very basic units or markings.

Meaning: The overall gestalt of this picture suggests a sun image. Disintegration of form is conveyed through the irregularity of each tiny individual component of the drawing, as well as the incomplete circular shape at the picture's center and the lack of symmetry in the radial formation. Poor form quality combined with a perseverative approach are typical of drawings by people with neurological impairment (Bender, 1952). This is why it is imperative that single works of art not be taken out of context of a body of work in practicing diagnostic assessment. The woman who drew this picture also drew Figure 4-7. The very qualities that might lead to an assessment of neurological impairment can be understood in the dissociative patient's work from a different perspective. The person going into trance is less likely to be aware of completing a gestalt or establishing symmetry in a picture, as she is in the midst of shifting states of awareness. One DID client said that when in this state "it feels like all the atoms are flying out of your body . . . you lose a sense of continuity and time."

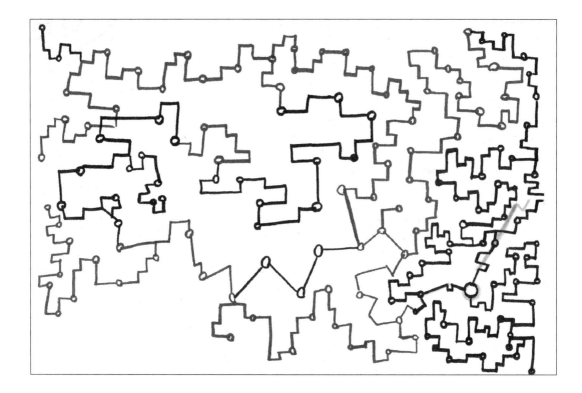

FIGURE 8-3

Structure: Small circles drawn in red and black are scattered randomly across the space. Each circle is connected to the next by straight and step-like red or black lines. There is no clear sequentiality to the resulting pattern, rather a complexity with no particular focal point. The largest circle in the picture, located in the lower right corner, is circumscribed with green. A green line extends diagonally upward from it.

Meaning: Reminiscent of a connect-the-dots picture, this example creates no recognizable image. There seems to be no special significance to the color changes, and the overall organization is poor despite a superficially structured gestalt. One is struck primarily by the maze- or circuit-like quality of this drawing. Its perseverative nature resembles the random but rigid doodling of an obsessive client. The woman who drew this picture reported using this graphic technique as a way to control the shift in mind states when an internal wave of chaos was encroaching.

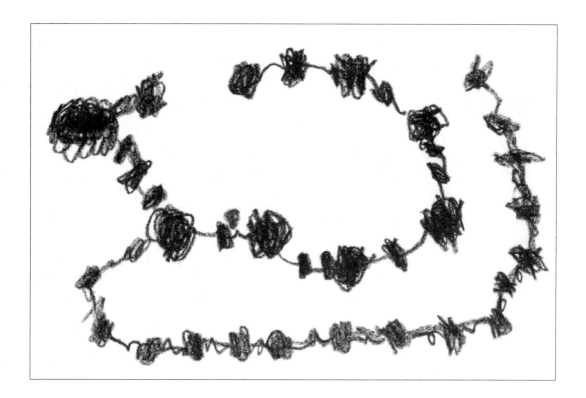

FIGURE 8-4

Structure: A series of irregularly shaped scribbles are sequentially placed across the page, connected by twisting lines. The monochromatic black configuration has no focal point. Drawn in crayon, these primitive markings vary primarily in size and pressure of application. A single triangular shape is outlined in yellow close to the center of the page.

Meaning: The irregular line quality coupled with the primitiveness of form in this drawing suggests the possibility of an organic disorder. It was drawn, in fact, by a child alter of the client who drew Figure 8-3, in an attempt to control state shifts. A younger hand (with less fine motor control) is evident.

FIGURE 8-5

Structure: Slightly curving black and white lines cover a page of blended rainbow colors, drawn in chalk pastel. Diffusion is the principal artmaking strategy employed; movement emanates toward all edges of the page. Close inspection reveals tiny black circles in the center right portion of the space, reinforcing the perseverative nature of this work.

Meaning: The atmospheric tone of this composition combined with the graceful flow of linear elements may evoke images of blowing grasses or falling rain; there is certainly a sense of freedom. In this instance, the process of making the artwork and the diffuse effect of the resulting image facilitate the client's shift into an altered state that is free-floating and without boundaries.

FIGURE 8-6

Structure: Pink and violet tempera paint are used to create a seamless labyrinth of looping lines. A small splatter of pink appears at the left center, while a seemingly more purposeful dot of purple is placed just below it. A single horizontal line painted in pink spans the width of the page at its bottom. Movement and randomness characterize this expressionist composition.

Meaning: There is nothing inherently pathological about this stereotypical doodle image; its color is vibrant, and its execution is energetic and direct. Only within the context of a body of work by a person with suspected MPD should this image prompt further exploration. In this instance, the meandering movement of the lines and fluidity of the paint facilitate a shift of consciousness.

FIGURE 8-7

Structure: A violet marker was used to draw a continuously spiraling line that coils around and around forming an overall circular gestalt. This configuration is placed to the far left of the page.

Meaning: A doodle such as this might be drawn by anyone in a somewhat trance-like state. The motor activity necessary to create continuously looping lines may itself facilitate a light hypnotic trance. This simple pattern illustrates the client's method of trance induction; its unusual placement testifies to the artist's relative lack of concern for the look of the product over the effect of the process.

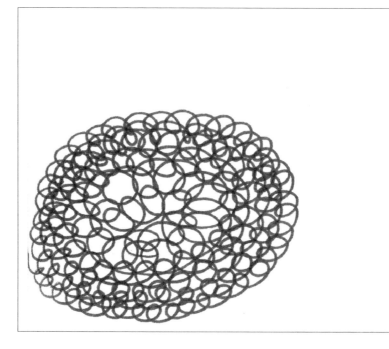

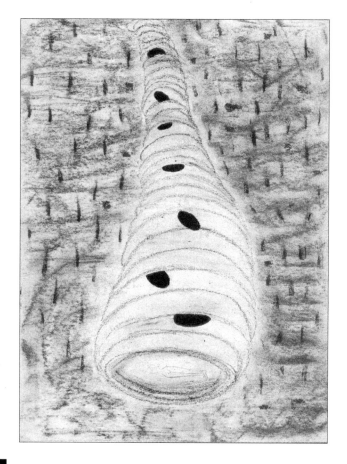

FIGURE 8-8

Structure: A tall violet funnel, wide at the bottom and narrow at the top, is centrally placed against a background of purple marked by vertical purple lines. Black oval shapes are sequentially placed along the length of the funnel's exterior, suggesting movement. The widening configuration of the central image further amplifies the illusion of motion. The lower half of a female figure is drawn in pencil within the elliptical base of the funnel.

Meaning: In the literature of art therapy downward spiraling configurations imply depression (Wadeson, 1980) and black and purple have been hypothesized to reflect feelings of loss (Kellogg, 1984). Although loss may indeed be one theme in this picture, another theme is addressed through the depiction of kinesthetic downward motion, suggesting entry into an altered state of consciousness. The perseverative markings in the background further reinforce this trance-inducing rhythm. Various versions of the spiral shape or its three-dimensional counterpart, the funnel, are frequently found in the drawings of individuals diagnosed with DID. This might possibly be related to the symbol's association with the hypnotic process (Cirlot, 1962; Kellogg, 1984).

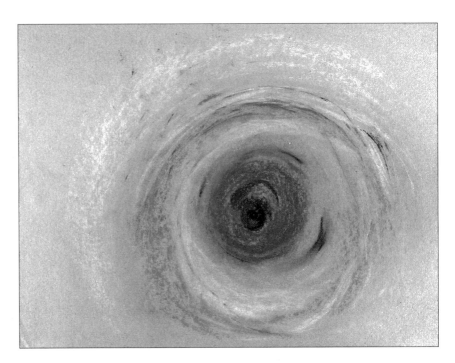

FIGURE 8-9

Structure: The media characteristics of chalk pastels are well utilized in this swirling image of blues, greys, and whites on dull grey paper. Color is saturated at the center of the picture and diffuse around its perimeter. The chalks are smeared, blended, and lightly applied. Color saturation and movement characterize expressionism, as it is used here in this abstract picture.

Meaning: The almost centripetal pull toward the center of this image might lead the viewer to perceive this elegant drawing as some sort of descent. Upon close examination, a tiny black figure (head and arms) seems to appear at the center of the composition. Pulling back and looking at this image from far away, a single eye stares back at the viewer. All of these various clues—the tiny figure, staring eye, and spiraling movement—lead the viewer to suspect dissociative trance induction coupled with multiplicity; this picture, nonetheless, remains highly obscure.

FIGURE 8-10

Structure: Short, broken lines are drawn in black marker to create a sequence of concentric rectangles. The overall pattern suggests movement in that the central markings are smaller, drawing the eye inward. Complexity of composition reinforces diffusion, since it is difficult to rest visually at any single point in the picture. The flatness nonetheless is characteristic of elementalism.

Meaning: The relative precision and perseveration evidenced in this picture might possibly represent the stereotypic work of a compulsive person with limited creativity. Meaning is obscure here, primarily because the process seems far more essential than the content to the artist at this moment. The effect is similar to op art of the 1960s, which itself induced shifts in the viewer's perception and mind state. It is conceivable that this overall pattern was executed as a defensive maneuver to ward off anxiety or keep others at a distance. Perseveration in this picture is linked to the dissociative defense, allowing its maker to shift states of consciousness and avoid unpleasant or anxiety-provoking stimuli.

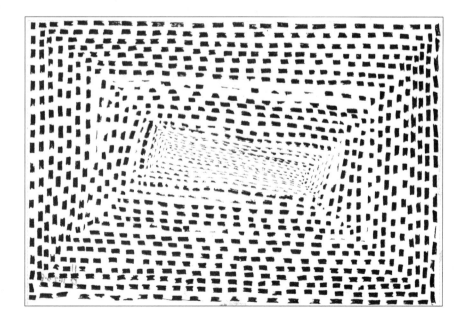

CHAPTER 8

FIGURE 8-11

Structure: The page is divided into three compositional sections in this drawing. Across the top of the page are randomly placed star shapes drawn in violet marker. Across the center, a complex array of small vertical marks are also drawn in violet, creating a diffuse effect. In the lower section, near the bottom of the page, a violet stick figure lies supine, its long hair flowing out and up from its crown. Across much of the page's surface is a swirling mass of pale blue lines drawn in chalk pastel, juxtaposing expressionist movement with elemental figuration.

Meaning: The ethereal, dreamlike quality of this drawing is the result of both the drawing media and the overall patterning achieved by the repetitive marks. Further, the central figure lies as if asleep at the base of the page, gazing upward at the stars. The varying sizes of the stars create visual movement and depth. All of these features support one another in transporting the viewer into a floating or trance-like state of mind.

What can the viewer make of this image, which contains both positively and negatively charged imagery? The colors suggest an airy, happy mood, as do the stars; the background resembles clouds, however, and the markings rain. The figure at the bottom of the page is not in reverie; she frowns and may even appear flattened by the downward movement above her. This dichotomy might be explained by the DID client's use of the artmaking to induce trance and shift states of consciousness. The process is recorded on paper through the media and the alteration in state is literally depicted, resulting in an image that reflects both "before" and "after."

Conclusion   Dots and dooodles are not usually scrutinized very closely by art therapists and are sometimes viewed as merely stereotypical or defensive in nature. Yet these drawings, while being the most rudimentary pictures of all those under consideration, reflect much about their makers.

The ubiquitous claim that "my kid can do that" is, in this case, quite true and that is just the point. The primitive markings that characterize elementalism link the behavior of the traumatized dissociative adult with childhood play. Rocking and twirling, for instance, are two developmentally early behaviors that can be used to maintain altered states of consciousness; they are the kinesthetic counterparts of the gestures seen in induction pictures. This rudimentary quality is primarily the result of the immediacy of mark-making that occurs during the trance induction process.

Induction pictures are either monochromatic (typically done in black) or feature a limited palette, since the dissociative client is in the process of shifting states of consciousness, when affect is usually minimal. It is striking how many of these images are rendered in violet; this may support one theory suggesting that violet reflects the quality of merging and lack of differentiation, "dissociation from the physical body" (Kellogg, 1984, p. 44). Blue is also commonly used in induction pictures, reinforcing notions of blue as having a physical quality that retreats or withdraws into itself.

Two images that sometimes stand in for the abstract patterns more typical of this category are stars (Figure 8-11) and bubbles (see Figure 13-10e). They suggest a free-floating quality regardless of their compositional organization. In another example, a client drew a floral wallpaper pattern into a picture to camouflage its traumatic-dissociative narrative (Figure 13-6c). Acoustic ceiling tile patterns and erratic woodgraining in wall paneling are effective as induction aids, according to many patients. They can be easily incorporated into drawings.

Although the vast majority of induction pictures seem to be highly random in their organization, perseverative activity accompanied by movement (like an insomniac counting sheep) helps one to shift mind states. Randomness and diffusion are strategies that visually reflect an internal state lacking order, boundaries, and focus. When movement is featured, expressionism is the typical style. However, elementalism, with its characteristic flatness and emphasis on bare essentials, is the style most often used in induction pictures.

Of all the pictures in the ten category model, induction pictures tend to be the most obscure. Unless you know you are looking at an induction picture, there is very little available to communicate meaning. Conversely, for the well-informed viewer, these perseverative marks tell one part of a story of survival achieved by the shifting of awareness. The induction, however, is only the preliminary step to the attainment of self-hypnotic trance in the face of overwhelming trauma or anxiety.

Chapter 9

Trance Pictures
Internal Realities

T he distortions of the dream world have long fascinated children and adults alike. Lewis Carroll's nineteenth-century masterworks of childhood literature, *Alice's Adventures in Wonderland* and *Through the Looking Glass*, are excellent resources for examples of trance imagery and situations. Those who have read or listened to these books or seen film adaptations retain vivid images of fluid changes in size, shifting reality orientations, condensations of humans with animals or inanimate objects, and the preoccupation with time; these archetypes revivify human conflicts and concerns in a most effective way. They are the stuff of trance pictures.

The young child's earliest mode of thinking has much in common with the topsy-turvy quality of dreams; Freud (1911) called this "primary process." Typified by a disregard for time and space, the structures of external reality, and the logic of rational thought, primary process is an essential component in dreams, children's play, and creativity.

Franklin (1990) hypothesizes that dreamlike thought process is necessary for the formation of alternate parts of self in severely traumatized children. She also points out the similarities in modes of mental processing between dreaming and hypnosis. Both share a characteristic called "trance logic" (Orne, 1959), in which the coexistence of incompatible images and experiences becomes possible and a variety of cognitive distortions are supported by the suspension of reality-testing. In this way, the child who is being abused can use her innate capacity for dissociation to escape to a personal reality in which painful and unacceptable stimuli can be segregated, stored, or reconfigured to defend against trauma (Franklin, 1990).

Trance pictures externalize the complex and disorienting inner experiences of the person with dissociative identity disorder. Art expression is the most effective vehicle for dissociative clients to share their inner worlds with their therapists, since writing and talking are by their nature ill-suited to communicating such information (Cohen, in press).

Trance pictures feature temporal condensation, coexistence of various types of perspective, combinations of elements from consensual reality, elements of fantasy, and situations that can best be described as uncommon or strange. Yet this is the everyday reality of the DID client, in which derealization, a feeling that the world and things in it are unreal, is common. A self-hypnotic regimen that facilitates automatic shifting among states of consciousness must therefore be maintained to sustain the dissociative reality. Habitual use of this defensive style results in its becoming "first nature" to the client.

Dissociative trance represents an extreme point along the same spectrum of experience as daydreaming. "Alternations of human awareness occur all the time," according to Spiegel and Spiegel (1978, p. 11); they emphasize the relationship between intense focus and decreased peripheral awareness during trance. Since there is no absolute dividing line between states of consciousness, one might argue that the DID client lives almost exclusively in trance, constantly shifting from one alter personality to another.

While the trance picture is in progress, images seem to flow in coded form, as in dreams. However, once the artist shifts out of the trance state, she may not retain any sense of authorship of the picture. Further, she is unlikely to understand its meaning due to the primary process qualities of the artwork and the effects of dissociative amnesia.

Even during times of waking consciousness, unbidden intrusions of autobiographical traumatic content may spontaneously recur as flashbacks. These waking nightmares are usually psychologically unmetabolized bits and pieces of memory that are, unfortunately, not dreams.

FIGURE 9-1

Structure: Purple marker was used to draw this complex picture, which juxtaposes dozens of small circular shapes with rudimentary images of faces, arrows, objects, and figures. At the lower left is a rectangle with three stick figures inside; another figure lies at the bottom of the page, while yet another stands below the image of a hatchet. Near the center of the page is a large face. Arrows imply movement and animate this complex and rather randomly organized composition.

Meaning: Perseveration, extreme generalization of form, and lack of thematic integration are immediately evident in this picture. Combining the above qualities with a linear execution and lack of color would lead the diagnostically-oriented observer to consider schizophrenia or some form of cognitive impairment in its maker (Cohen et al., 1988). In actuality, the unbidden graphic images of trauma, as seen in the activity between two adults and a child in the bed at the lower left, elicit the need to shift to another state, and the induction is set into motion. Alter personalities are depicted as jagged-edged entities with eyes. Arrows suggest a sequence of psychic response. The person who drew this picture was still unable to decode its obscure references beyond this level, despite five years of distance from its creation. Although this picture contains the perseverative quality of induction, the increased specificity of imagery distinguishes it as a trance picture.

FIGURE 9-2

Structure: Meticulously painted in watercolor, the figure of a nearly nude woman floats mid-page, her hair cascading downward. A tree with multiple holes, broken branches, and bared roots stands between the figure and a circular configuration whose surface is marked with a network of irregular jagged lines on the left, and spiraling lines emanating from a disembodied eye on the right. This section of the picture is primarily pink and blue. Leaves and droplets fall to the ground below the figure, creating a sense of movement. The juxtaposition of the various images, combined with the distortion of their relative scale, keeps the viewer's eye moving around this complex composition, resulting in a surreal style.

Meaning: There is no mistaking the dream-like quality of this image; a levitating woman whose eyes, drawn in cruciform configuration, suggest an altered state of consciousness. A single dark red drop connects the visual space between the figure and the floating eye in the upper right corner, also drawn in red. The spiral lines that emanate from the eye reinforce the hypnotic quality of this picture, while the cracked eggshell-like surface on the left suggests fragmentation, as do the scattered leaves. The perseverative nature of the falling droplets and leaves may have served the artist as induction into a trance state. The tree and female figure paradoxically seem both dead and alive. While the "bodies" of each are grey and lifeless, the dense clusters of leaves and the flowing yellow tresses indicate vitality. Although the long horizontal root of the tree implies a groundline, the entire image floats in a white void.

A decade or more ago the presence of the disembodied eye would have suggested paranoia (Dax, 1953) and teardrops depression, especially in an artwork that included a spiral-like form (Wadeson, 1980). Disembodied eyes have also recently been associated with the artwork of sexually traumatized women (Spring, 1993). For persons with dissociative identity disorder, eyes may represent internal observer entities or abusers. Although each individual element of this composition carries a particular meaning within the totality of this patient's work, the complex combination inhibits clear communication.

FIGURE 9-3

Structure: A colorful pictogram of simple designs conveys a subtle sense of movement through its undulating lines and shapes. An angular form encloses a design in red, black, and yellow, prominent in color and contrasting in configuration. A biomorphic green triangle encloses a yellow stick figure. On the right, a violet configuration has about six projections on each of its sides; golden yellow marks punctuate the tip of each. The flat, simplified elements in this painting are often seen in art made in the elemental style.

Meaning: Who among us has never doodled such a decorative page of squiggles and swirls? The angular black diamond shape with its not-so-concealed red eyes sounds a somewhat alarming note amidst the otherwise carnival coloring of this painting. With this in mind, the lumpy green wedge can be more clearly understood as an enclosure or container for the yellow stick figure. Between these two larger shapes is a fallen leaf shape enclosing an orange mark, which might also represent a disembodied eye. This painting alone would not indicate dissociation or multiplicity. However, the emphasis on corner placement and enclosed configurations has previously been noted in the art of those diagnosed with MPD (Mills & Cohen, 1993). The repetition of simple forms also suggests the transition from the perseveration of induction to the primary process imagery of trance. Even though this painting was made by a woman diagnosed with MPD, it alone is not sufficient for identifying multiplicity. In any case, recognized or not as a painting by a DID client, its meaning remains obscure.

FIGURE 9-4

Structure: There is no central focus in this randomly organized colored marker drawing. Its images are placed around the four edges of the page. Only a distorted pink face in the lower center part of the page is clearly representational. Perseverative lines, both vertical and horizontal, are juxtaposed with geometric doodles and highly personalized visual shorthand. There are references to both elementalism and surrealism in this drawing.

Meaning: When compared with Figure 9-3, this drawing done largely in similar colors is as obscure, and its markings, stark and geometric, are less cordial. The small image in the lower left corner suggests a group of figures. Above it, the configuration resembles a volcano. In both cases the coloring is idiosyncratic. In any case, like Figure 9-3, one can observe the graphic transition between the perseverative induction markings across the top and the subsequent altered state of consciousness evidenced in this drawing.

FIGURE 9-5

Structure: A hillside landscape is juxtaposed with distorted images of a handless clock and compass, a mirror, a pointing hand, and a black shape. An opening in the hill pours red color. The word "screw" is printed in mirror image in the sky above the horizon. The corner of a building can be seen at the upper right.

Meaning: Stark environs are offset by the bright red color that flows from the hillside, suggesting intense affect. The black pit compounds the emptiness of the scene, as does the nondescript building at the upper edge of the composition. Disorientation regarding time and space is loosely suggested by the pointing hand and the handless clock and compass. The empty mirror further expands the theme to issues of identity. The irrational narrative here could suggest psychosis, but the bold use of black and red linked with the mirror handwriting are important clues to trauma and dissociation in art productions. Blood is frequently employed in the artwork of people with DID to denote physical or emotional pain. Disorientation to time, place, and identity is endemic to individuals with multiple personality disorder as well. The word "screw" was written by an alter personality and probably represents switching from the sure-handed personality state in which the rest of the picture was drawn.

FIGURE 9-6

Structure: This picture is boldly drawn in colored pencils. A woman's face is the central image in a connected series of body parts that create a visual enclosure. The white of the paper used as the skin area of the face becomes deep space above the woodgrain design and below the mouth. Nine fingers and a thumb are wrapped around the blade of a dagger (from below) or knife (from above), the bottom of which is a human foot. A plant grows out of the upper right corner of the configuration. The space between the fingers and the female face is dark and also functions as a man's face in profile. The overall effect of these juxtapositions is a surrealistic portrait.

Meaning: The woman's face, framed by a 1930s hairstyle, stares out grimly at the viewer. Her image is intruded upon by the dark side or male profile who shares her lips. Nine fingers suggest more than one person's hands, yet she appears to grasp the handle firmly. The foot on the wooden floor is evocative of both the approaching perpetrator and the dissociative phenomenon in which the victim merges into the grain pattern of woodwork in order to escape trauma. The trajectory of the wedge shape that emanates from the foot leads into the plant form, a symbol of self for many people with MPD.

As with other trance pictures, this rather bizarre series of juxtapositions might have easily been labeled the work of a person with schizophrenia. In fact, this drawing was made by an adult client when she was hospitalized at age 14 with that diagnosis. If only therapists knew three decades ago what they know now, youngsters like this would possibly have been spared years of inappropriate and ineffective treatment.

(DREAM IMAGE)* 1995 7/15

FIGURE 9-7 **Structure:** A variety of colors, shapes, and images vie for the viewer's attention in this complex composition. Rendered in colored pencils, a bird lies at the center of the page, juxtaposed with the orange-colored profile of a woman's breasts, dripping red; above this is the split image of a face, its features distorted in size; reaching into that image is a transparently drawn cloaked figure, its arm outstretched; superimposed over that image is a hand, as large as the adult figure it covers; a diagonal red line connects it to the edge of the page with another red shape. The left side of the page is dominated by a tall green clocktower, dark clouds, and an ambiguous arrangement of shapes that seems to be a bed with a biomorphic red shape below its yellow pillows. The entire background of the picture is colored in pink. The multiple juxtapositions, mixed perspective vantages, and irrational situations are, of course, hallmarks of the surrealist style.

Meaning: The fractured female face at the top center of the page might have been, at one time, thought to describe the "split personality" of the schizophrenic. In the modern era of antipsychotic medications, however, images such as this one are hardly seen outside the highly traumatized population. Painful themes such as the cut hand, bleeding bed, dead bird, and breasts oozing blood are indicative of trauma. Further, the "poisoned milk" of the breasts suggests an intrafamilial link. Likewise, the reference to time—especially in its sharp and aggressive looking phallic clocktower form—is worthy of notice. The author of this picture titled it "Dream Image"; the dreamlike time-space distortion in this irrational composition is typical of trance pictures.

FIGURE 9-8 **Structure:** Abstract and representational images are commingled in this random composition drawn with colored pencils. The full-length dark blue female figure is juxtaposed with a horse's head; the relationship in scale between the two is emphasized. An abstracted biomorphic configuration (also drawn in blue) links the two visually. Several other elements float around the periphery of the page: three red wavy lines (each accompanied by a pattern of dots), a small grotesque brown face with blue hair, a disembodied stylized eye, and a distorted creature drawn in red and yellow.

Meaning: Set against a background of pale blue, these disjointed floating images remain nonetheless devoid of context and associated meaning. The transparency of the biomorphically shaped blue form (a humanoid figure on a pedestal) and the overall disconnection in this picture suggest the disintegrated quality in the art of thought disorder patients (Wadeson, 1980). Since the juxtaposition of forms is emphasized with imagery that is flagrantly irrational, the viewer is reminded to consider the artmaking strategies employed in surrealism, which is typical of trance pictures. However, all such art should not be assumed to be the product of dissociative makers. In the absence of explicit traumatic content, these free-association pictures must be carefully evaluated within the overall context of the patient's art.

FIGURE 9-9

Structure: In this boldly drawn composition, which is executed solely in black marker, an array of geometric and biomorphic shapes are placed amidst human figures, landscapes, and other ambiguous stimuli. Scale is exaggerated by the proximity of images; a snake, for instance, is taller than the full-length figure next to it. Similarly, the suggestion of deep space is achieved by the diminution of buildings and people that can be viewed through angular openings in the visual field, complemented by the dimensionality created with the use of crosshatching and shading. Movement is depicted through the positioning of a body with flexed limbs as well as flowing abstract forms. Juxtaposition of structural and narrative elements fosters compositional randomness in this surrealistic picture.

Meaning: Confusion comes to mind in response to the irrational contexts and complicated references in this drawing. In fact, this composition is only a detail from a much larger, more complex drawing. The mixture of vantages, sizes, content, and strategies used indicates a shifting of mind states, much like those encountered in the art of psychedelic drug users. However, drug-influenced art is almost always colorful. An extraordinary visual stream of consciousness (with no apparent narrative thread) and the over-articulation of space result in a claustrophobic sense, which can sometimes be found in the art of psychotic persons. The viewer is challenged to draw upon personal associations to these striking images in order to construct meaning from them; consequently, a reading of the picture's message would be largely based on the projections of the viewer, rather than the intended communication of the artist. This compelling example, drawn by a man with post-traumatic dissociation, includes all of the typical features of a trance picture.

FIGURE 9-10 **Structure:** A pen and ink drawing features a complex array of images, juxtaposed in novel and surprising ways. Somewhat centrally placed in this drawing is the blindfolded face of a woman, partially hidden by the roof of a house, which is also a razor blade. The corners of the house are pinned down; the windows are dark. A chain is connected at one end to the roof by a safety pin and at the other end to a ring pierced through a tombstone. "R.I.P." is the upside-down epitaph on it; a hat rests at its base. Severed fingers and a tiny leg are wrapped in the roots of a flower, the long stem of which moves upward to the top of the page. A hammer, smaller than the flower, as large as the house, hangs poised in mid-air above it. A pair of feet move downward at the top of the page; they are seen from below—an out-of-body perspective. A pigtailed girl's head hangs down below the feet, dwarfed by their exaggerated size. "MOMMA" is written in rounded dimensional letters; droplets fall from them into shapes on the ground. A long, winding road brings the viewer's eye back to the foreground of the picture, over a bridge, to a key which is as large as the house itself.

Meaning: This drawing is an excellent example of an extraordinarily complicated and multileveled trance picture. In addition to the characteristic distortion of scale and stream of consciousness imagery, certain components communicate more than one manifest level of meaning. The house, for instance, as a symbol of self (in relation to family of origin) is pierced, pinned down, chained to a tombstone, dark, empty, and has a razor blade for a roof. The blood dripping from "MOMMA" falls into pools, which are also army tanks. The "key" to all of this is concretely depicted in the lower right but, held down by a wire, is rendered useless. Two themes predominate in this picture: dissociation and mutilation. Dissociation as it relates to escape is suggested by the house, which is ready to float away; the oversized feet hovering above the picture; and the upside-down suspended girl. Mutilation is represented by the severed fingers, the razor blade, and the sharp pins. Additionally, many of the images in this drawing are restrained in some way, much as the woman's eyes are blindfolded. The latter theme distinguishes this jumble of images from those drawn by psychotic individuals; along with the former two themes, it highlights central issues for the severely abused client.

FIGURE 9-11

Structure: A highly complex pen and ink drawing has at its center a profile portrait of an adult. A large snake, several partial faces, stick figures, leaves, checkerboard, stairs, electric plug, light fixture, and animal heads are randomly juxtaposed across the entire page. The word "unsafe" is boldly written across the blade of a knife. Scale is exaggerated throughout the composition by enlarging and shrinking sizes. These artmaking strategies, combined with irrationally juxtaposed content, are typical of the surrealistic style.

Meaning: Jumbled into this composition are an array of human, animal, and inanimate objects whose thematic relationships suggest danger, conflict, pain, and vulnerability. This initially confusing array of imagery is reminiscent of the "picture salad" productions of psychotic patients. However, the out-of-body perspective looking down on the child's head, seen at the lower right, coupled with the extreme exploitation of scale, leads the viewer to suspect a dissociative process. Psychotic art more typically includes a variety of loosely related images placed with equal emphasis on the page. The trance picture, however, often builds on a theme or image in a deceptively organized fashion, linking signifiers of events to reactions. In this drawing, issues of safety in the world, as well as within the system, are of key concern. This would be the case even if the word "unsafe" were deleted from the drawn image. Specific meanings of individual images remain primarily obscure, even from the artist.

Conclusion Disparate combinations of content and disjunctive compositions found in trance pictures parallel the experience of the trauma victim. Trauma, as defined by Spiegel (1991), represents a "sudden discontinuity in physical and psychological experience," thus the isomorphic parallel between the ordeal and its graphic representation. Further, over time, the frequency with which dissociative states of consciousness are accessed increases. As mentioned previously, irrational, atemporal, and nonlinear constructs are fostered in this hypnoid state (Horowitz, 1970). Their only efficient outlet for expression, hence communication, is through art. Surrealism is the style that best suits these phenomena (Cohen, in press).

The seemingly haphazard arrangement of elements, juxtaposition of ostensibly unrelated images, and manipulation of form and scale foster the dreamlike contexts typical of trance pictures. Randomness, an artmaking strategy essential to these artworks, functions differently in trance pictures than it does in induction pictures. In the former, the placement of markings is largely arbitrary, owing primarily to the gestural action of the hand. The latter features randomness of a more calculated nature (mindfulness during disorientation being a somewhat paradoxical notion except during dissociation), as parallel consciousness performs multiple tasks that simultaneously reveal and conceal meaning.

Juxtaposition of disparate elements is quintessential surrealism; Lautréamont, a French author to whom the surrealists looked for inspiration, is often noted for writing, "beautiful as the chance encounter of a sewing machine and an umbrella on an operating table" (cited in Murray & Murray, 1959, p. 311). This accurately describes the juxtaposition of elements that typifies trance pictures. It is important to recognize the distinction between the use of juxtaposition in this category and in barrier pictures. Barrier pictures employ juxtaposition to compare or segregate two or more images. Juxtaposition in trance pictures joins divergent subjects in order to suggest a hidden relationship and simultaneously disarm the viewer.

In trance pictures, distortions and exaggerations help to illustrate shifting points of perspective and reference; a household key, for instance, looms as large as a house in one of these surrealist images (Figure 9-10). Manipulations of form are also used in expressionist imagery, but to heighten emotional impact rather than disorient through spatial relationships. Color in trance pictures denotes affect that has surfaced into consciousness. This is often the exception rather than the rule, since trance pictures are not primarily concerned with affect; thus, color does not play a central role.

Trance pictures are most notably of help in the communication of unspeakable or cognitively untranslatable schemas, and therefore contain information of a highly obscure nature. For this reason, their meaning may not become apparent or fully decoded except through extensive hypnotherapy and long-term psychotherapy.

The obscure graphic productions of individuals with thought disorders differ from trance pictures in a variety of ways. A discussion with the artist is often the simplest way to discern one from the other; the schizophrenic patient will typically confabulate an explanation regarding a picture with themes of a delusional or grandiose nature. DID patients will either "not know" the meaning of their pictures, not remember making them, or proffer a socially appropriate description as a cover-up. Their themes are more typically self-referential and personally idiosyncratic, owing to their propensity for multileveledness and coding.

As the patient drifts psychologically through the visual flotsam and jetsam of verbally unprocessed material, particular images connect and rekindle affectively charged clusters of experience fragments. When sufficient links are established intrapsychically, dissociated material may be recalled into awareness. Then the pressure for abreactive discharge builds.

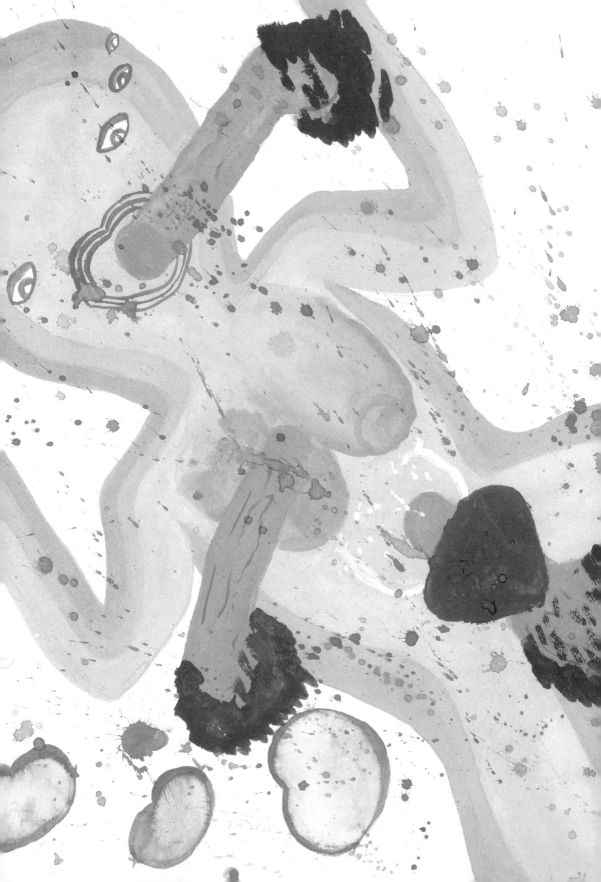

Chapter 10

Abreaction Pictures
Traumatic Experience Revisited

A nyone can forget details that are unnecessary or unimportant; some people have difficulty with significant information, new information, or information from long ago. But what if you had no recall of the last few hours, days, or months? What if you had no memory whatsoever of your childhood prior to adolescence? This is not uncommon for the person with dissociative identity disorder. "Amnesia or 'time loss' is the single most common dissociative symptom in MPD patients" (Putnam, 1989, p. 59).

Some things are best forgotten, particularly when they are unpleasant, painful, or traumatic. Dissociative amnesia, however, can take everything along with it—not just a bad memory, but an entire life's history. The amnestic barriers discussed in Chapter 6 often compartmentalize intolerable and unprocessed bits of traumatic experience; they prevent information from leaking out into conscious awareness while they protect against incoming anxiety-provoking experiences. For this reason, the person with dissociative identity disorder might be unable both to remember and to forget.

Since the return of the veterans from Vietnam, the public has become increasingly familiar with the long-term effects of post-traumatic stress. Many have become all too familiar with stories of the physiologically-based startle response; a loud sound in the night leads a veteran to grab for his rifle, scream, and "hit the dirt." Flashbacks, in which the trauma survivor is jolted into re-experiencing the original situation at all levels of bodily and psychological experience, are triggered by environmental cues—sights, sounds, smells, tastes, touches, and situations. This keeps the survivors of acute trauma hooked to a tether of revivification that is difficult to sever.

The earlier the abuse, the more chronic the symptoms; the more insidious and sadistic the abuse, the greater the need for dissociation as a defense. Fluctuation between the extremes of constriction (numbing of feeling and thought) and hyperarousal (flooding of affect and somatic sensation) illustrates the simultaneously defensive and defenseless position of the person with severe post-traumatic stress.

When the fragments of experience surface in dreams, trance, or waking consciousness, they may connect with related fragments into clusters. As psychic energy is released through the unlocking of amnestic chains, related information, feelings, somatic sensations, and actions begin to take the form of remembered experience. As this occurs, psychic energy often continues to increase and to become evident in several ways in the person's daily life.

Braun (1988) has developed a model that helps to simplify and explain this experience. The BASK model, as it is called, describes the conditions that comprise mental health. Braun posits that positive mental health is achieved when a person's *behavior*, *affect*, *sensations*, and *knowledge* are congruent with each other and confluent over time. When one or more of the four BASK components or levels is blocked or split off from the others, the person's behavior eventually becomes dysfunctional. The broader the cleft between the disconnected level and the others, the more extensive the dysfunction becomes. When more than one level is blocked, difficulties are multiplied.

Consider, for example, what might happen when affect and sensation are detached from behavior and knowledge. In an instance of physical abuse or self-mutilation, neither sensate nor emotional feelings would be engaged, allowing for the continued behavior despite cognitive awareness of its potential for long-term physical or psychological damage. On the contrary, the presence of sensation and affect without knowledge or behavior leaves the person completely overwhelmed by feelings and flooded with somatic stimuli.

Artwork is a splendid vehicle for observing these dynamics, as Fuhrman (1993) has discussed. Each level of the BASK model may be clearly delineated in drawings; further, it is not uncommon for particular alters of DID patients to perform distinct functions and, consequently, hold specific pieces of the BASK. Their discrete concerns can be communicated graphically, verbally in therapy, and pictorially in art.

Abreaction pictures that feature one of the BASK levels typically display characteristic themes. For the most part, these include alarming portrayals of a violent, sexual, and sadistic nature. Those that deal with behaviors usually illustrate situations and responses to show "what happened." Sometimes the artist will assume a particular posture or re-enact the incident upon externalizing it in the picture. Abreaction pictures in which affect predominates usually depict crying, screaming, or extreme terror. The artmaking strategies and styles used to create these images are essential to their effective communication.

Most abreaction pictures that focus on a single BASK level are predominantly concerned with sensation. These drawings employ a narrative approach combined with the strategic use of color to show "how it felt." Unlike pictures that focus on affect, which use color to set a feeling tone, pictures about sensation feature color (usually red) to signify physical pain. Body memories—the spontaneous recurrence of somatic sensations much like visual flashbacks—are among the more exasperating symptoms of this disorder. Art allows expression of those memories. Knowledge is communicated in pictures through the depiction of particular information, clues to the patients' biographical mysteries. In this sense, these pictures are often about "whodunit."

FIGURE 10-1 **Structure:** In this naturalistic pen and ink drawing, a young girl sits atop a cube, her head bowed and legs crossed at the ankles. Her hands are tucked beneath her. On the ground behind her are a pair of scissors and two lengths of braided hair. To the far right a door stands open leading into darkness. There are no other environmental elements in this picture; not even a groundline is denoted.

Meaning: The narrative aspect of this picture communicates clearly, as the storytelling elements have been pared down to the essentials. Isolation and loneliness are suggested by the emptiness of the environment. The darkness beyond the open door is ominous; one cannot be certain that the offender will not return. The girl is physically closed in upon herself and her bowed head communicates dejection or sadness within a stark setting sharply delineated in black and white. This postural behavior is frequently observed among adult survivors of abuse, often in a more extreme manifestation in which the upper torso is collapsed, the eyes closed, and the limbs brought inward (Simonds, 1994).

FIGURE 10-2

Structure: Drawn primarily in the lower left corner of the page, two jagged black forms create a zigzag white space between them. A curved oblong shape, drawn in purple just to the right of the white line at the bottom of the page, is covered with orange dots and outlined in white. The remainder of this marker drawing is blank. The simplicity and boldness of this elemental composition allow the viewer to focus on the juxtaposition of the two primary shapes.

Meaning: This drawing is so highly stylized and visually flat that the unsuspecting viewer might see it initially as an abstraction. Upon closer scrutiny, a crouching fetal figure is seen beneath a flight of stairs. The placement of the image in the corner of the page reinforces the theme of hiding, and the high contrast of the black and white communicates the intensity of the experience, while the darkness emphasizes isolation. The lack of definition of the body portrays both the helplessness and worthlessness of the subject. These feelings are characteristic of individuals with depression; however, it is the activity of hiding that distinguishes the severely abused client. The woman who drew this picture stated that the fetal schema is one that she uses to represent an alter who primarily engaged in hiding behavior either before or after an incident of abuse at home. As an adult this individual still finds herself on the floor of her closet at home. Another representation of this alter personality can be seen in Figure 11-11.

FIGURE 10-3 **Structure:** In this expressionistic tempera painting a stylized white face is pasted onto a painted black background. Red is daubed over the perimeter of the image and cascades downward, where it covers a pair of collaged, detached hands. Boldness and exaggeration further heighten the expression on the face, which is drawn simply in black marker.

Meaning: The visceral impact of this image is difficult to avoid. Various artmaking strategies combine to enhance the terror personified here. The viewer is reminded of Munch's familiar painting "The Scream." In artmaking, the silenced child is afforded a venue in which to express extreme affect even when sounds or words are not available. The colors red, black, and white heighten the expression of emotion in this picture.

FIGURE 10-4 **Structure:** Three human figures are drawn in black crayon in this narrative picture. A small figure is supine on a surface that is delineated, but spatially ambiguous. Red dots are adjacent to the face and a single black line is perpendicular to each extremity. The larger figures are connected to the smaller figure and one holds a long red shape. Red and yellow markings float along the left edge of the page, which has been torn by the client.

Meaning: One is struck by the crude drawing style and elementary level of graphic development of this picture fragment, which might have been drawn by a child and was, in fact, drawn by a child alter personality of an adult patient with MPD. It depicts two anonymous adult figures restraining a child, whose arms and legs have been strapped down to what appears to be a table. The figure on the right seems to be holding an implement of some sort, red or covered in blood, in proximity to her genital area. The artist herself identified the floating objects at the left as candles. Despite the ambiguities of this drawing, the attention to detail on the head of the child is noteworthy. Hair is included on this figure only, a frown is clearly delineated, and red tears fall from the face. The color of the tears may connect visually with the red weapon in the hand of the abuser. This minimal but highly effective use of color heightens the affect of sadness and the sensation of pain. The torn paper is a product of the conflicts regarding the depicted event and its externalization through art.

FIGURE 10-5

Structure: A pink stick figure is drawn in oil pastel at the upper left corner of the page; a purple line zigzags diagonally from below the figure down to the lower right corner. Seven solid red circles are sequentially drawn left to right, from smallest to largest, on the horizontal line of each angle. Movement is thus suggested by the exaggeration of size across the series of circles. The remainder of the page is blank.

Meaning: The posture of the stick figure, with its arms and legs raised, suggests the potential for movement. The horizontal line atop the head is unspecific in nature. The red circular forms might represent a ball rolling down the stairs, yet the increase in scale is perplexing. How do these images relate to one another? At first look, the poverty of content coupled with the apparently unrelated images and the elemental linear execution might suggest the work of a chronic schizophrenic. The strongest feature in the drawing seems to be the red shape; red is frequently used by dissociative clients to denote pain (and often anger). Connected with the odd line above the figure's head, the momentum suggested by the growing size of the red mark as it rolls downward provides a cogent explanation for this picture. The artist has, in a rather sophisticated manner, illustrated the memory of the sensation of falling down the stairs. The line adjacent to the head indicates a site of physical impact.

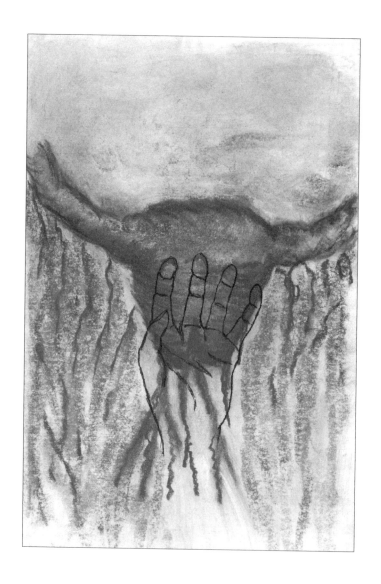

FIGURE 10-6   **Structure:** Chalk pastel is the primary media used to execute this picture, which features the central image of a hand reaching upward. A large bulbous red shape with bilateral tubular projections is seen through the transparent hand, which is drawn in marker. Irregular bands of yellow and orange cover the page on both sides of the hand. Deep red lines are drawn over the palm of the hand, originating at the bottom of the large red shape. Red chalk dust is smeared across the top half of the page. Expressionism is used to emphasize the impact of the imagery through scale and use of color. **Meaning:** The combination of the color and biomorphic shape in this drawing quickly communicates a painful physiological experience. The red bull's head shape, suggestive of a uterus, is centrally placed, amplified by color and intensity of application. The fingers of the hand are bent as if to grab or claw. Red blood streams down in rivulets over the hand, while around it the yellow, orange, and red suggest intense sensation, such as heat or pain. There is a paradoxical calm in the pink upper half of the page; it is detached from the fiery imagery below it. This is perhaps the only indicator of dissociation in this excruciatingly explicit picture. The woman who drew it called upon a variety of artmaking strategies to enhance her message.

FIGURE 10-7

Structure: Tempera paints were used to create this image of a woman's nude figure surrounded by disembodied penises. The figure is outlined in successively darker bands of color. Red and pink paint is splashed between the figure's splayed legs and splattered across the picture's surface. Three biomorphic shapes float in the lower left corner of the page; outlined in red, their interiors are pink. At the very center of the painting is a flat black triangle that appears to be attached to the surface of the picture. In the lower right corner, a tiny red figure is surrounded by red paint, which is enclosed in an oval of white. Movement, boldness, distortion, and polychrome are used in a way that is characteristic of expressionism.

Meaning: Despite the somewhat bizarre aspects of this image, one is immediately hit by the raw sexuality of its subject matter and the strength of its execution. Splatters of red keep the eye moving across the page's surface, while the four fleshy penises with their coal black pubic hair add to the compositional distraction. More subtle, however, are the four sets of three images that occur. Most obvious of these are the three sets of eyes that decrease in size, suggesting perspective. These correspond with the bands of color that outline the nude figure and draw attention to the triple mouth outline on the face. One might then assume that the biomorphic shapes in the left corner are disembodied mouths. Black appears to be used to denote pubic hair throughout the painting, which explains the central bold triangle. Vaginal penetration is seen in x-ray (typical of children and psychotics), blood flowing red from the woman and white sperm ejaculating from the penis. These factors give us many clues, but few certainties. The meaning at the level of the rape is clear, beyond that, ambiguous. Are the numbers of sex organs and the wild intensity the product of a hypersexual obsession or manic delusion? Clarity of meaning lies in the groupings of threes. Painted by a woman with DID who was gang raped during a psychiatric hospitalization, the silhouettes, eyes, and mouths describe the alternation among personalities in response to the overwhelming nature of this adult onset trauma. One can only speculate as to the intended meaning of the tiny figure in the lower corner of the page. Sensation is the primary focus of this abreaction picture. (See Figure 12-1 by this client for a related picture.)

FIGURE 10-8 **Structure:** A full-length portrait of a nun in habit is drawn in black marker; her hands are red. Around her are a pair of scissors, a knife, pins, needle and thread, and a spool of thread. A coiled length of interlocking circles resembles a chain. A church floats in the upper right corner. The drawing is detailed, executed in a clear and direct manner. The sister's name (deleted from the reproduction) was written below the figure.

Meaning: The frowning expression on this nun's face is echoed in the rigid down-turned configuration of her veil. Her stance is also rigid, reinforced by the vertical panel on her habit. She is surrounded by floating images of utensils, yet their purpose and relationship to her are not clear; while the items on the right of the picture are for mending, those on the left are potentially destructive. Her connection to the church itself is rather tenuous as it is depicted here. The building seems to levitate off the corner of the page. A subtle anthropomorphic stare is suggested by the round windows and blank entryway. It is the color of her hands that alerts the viewer to the unexpected message in this drawing. This image was one in a series of pictures executed in an attempt to master traumatic memories of molestation during the client's adolescent years in a foreign convent. The sewing accoutrements refer to her activity at the time of her traumatization. This picture completed her knowledge about the abuse, in that she depicts and names the perpetrator and links the trauma contextually to her interrupted sewing activity.

FIGURE 10-9a

FIGURE 10-9b

FIGURE 10-9

Structure: A simply drawn face is outlined by an irregular purple line; the facial features are denoted by small lines and compact shapes. Five large elliptical shapes outlined in red and filled in with purple overlap the top half of the face, each one connected to a single purple line. The schema is bold and simple, expressionistic in the distortion of the face's outline. The rest of the page is blank.

Meaning: There is an exotic look to this mask-like image, with its narrow slit eyes and feline nose. A headdress reminiscent of Medusa or an elaborate contraption of electrodes with leads are suggested, but only ambiguously. However, the creation of Figure 10-9b helped to explain the memory that began to emerge in Figure 10-9a. At the age of approximately eight, this woman was tied by her mother to a pole in the broom closet where rats ran across her body. Whereas Figure 10-9a represents the sensation component of her memory of the rats sniffing about her face, drawn by a child alter, Figure 10-9b is the adult woman's knowledge component illustrating the memory as a complete event. The latter picture is more naturalistic and includes an environmental context, whereas the former focuses exclusively on the physical experience.

FIGURE 10-10a

FIGURE 10-10b

FIGURE 10-10 **Structure:** A naked infant is seem from above. Drawn in black chalk pastel, its features are all but obscured by curving lines of red, blended with yellow, blue, and pink, which emanate from between its legs. The rest of the page is blank, allowing the boldly drawn image with the upward moving colors to clearly communicate its message.

Meaning: The shocking and confrontational image in Figure 10-10a suggests a plant, fountain, or fire rising from the crotch of the rounded infant's body. Readers of this book have by now seen numerous images of red and have been alerted to its message of pain. Drawn by the same client who drew Figure 10-6, this graphic image gives the viewer little psychic distance for cognitive escape. As for a child trapped in an abusive situation, the only way out is through dissociation. This picture, however, concretizes sensation, which is explained more fully as knowledge in Figure 10-10b. Here the memory of sexual violation of the female baby self by the adult male uncle is recorded. The somatic memory was quite potent for this woman. Such severe body flashbacks are a phenomenon that must be addressed by those who question the veracity of so-called "recovered memories" of early childhood trauma.

Conclusion   For dissociative patients traumatic material may suddenly recur on several levels of behavior, affect, sensation, and knowledge simultaneously. What makes this phenomenon so powerful to experience and daunting to cope with is the way it compromises the present for the patient, replacing it with details from the past. Friends standing nearby may "become" abusers, ordinary objects at hand may serve as stand-ins for implements of violence, and a workplace may be experienced as the childhood nursery. What must be understood is that the here-and-now is completely usurped, as if in a time warp, including all aspects of physical, emotional, sensory, and cognitive functioning.

When they occur spontaneously, abreaction pictures may carry all the impact of full physical revivification; when properly planned, they offer an opportunity for externalization that is safely distanced from the possibility of retraumatization. Used as a mediator of traumatic re-experiencing, abreaction pictures can provide an effective crucible for the psychic release of tensions; used as assigned tasks, they enable the separation and exploration of specific BASK components.

Of the four styles of art discussed in this book, only surrealism is unlikely to be used in an abreaction picture. This is because surrealism is primarily a stylistic vehicle for the concretization of trance. Although abreactions certainly take place in trance, the narrative nature of these drawings is incompatible with the disjunctive quality of trance pictures. Expressionism, in fact, is the style most likely to be used in drawing abreactive imagery, due to the intense level of physical and psychological energy that is stirred up and released in the process. Consequently, exaggeration, distortion, and movement are common. Distortion and exaggeration amplify the sensate and affect-laden aspects of abreaction. Movement helps to illustrate the dramatic and narrative components, in addition to capturing a sense of immediacy. Red and black are also frequently used to reflect psychological and physiological pain, as well as rage and depression.

When young part-selves are drawing, and in instances when coding is necessary to conceal what has inadvertently been revealed, elementalism may be used. These drawings tend to feature boldness and simplicity in communicating their messages. Simplicity is a strategy typically used to illustrate a single aspect of the trauma or when the event is depicted from a child part's perspective. Boldness is a way to communicate the intensity of the incident. Naturalism, of course, is the sensible choice when clarity of knowledge is possible.

Abreaction pictures, like abreactions, are not in and of themselves therapeutic. Patients and therapists alike often fail to adequately process these relived memories and their component parts; this is crucial to the resolution of such painful intrusions from the past. Therapists must carefully work through clusters of memories according to each of the four BASK levels, assist the patient to synthesize what is gleaned, and assimilate the newly processed information in an adult cognitive mode. The goal here is to detoxify and dissipate the extraordinary energy embodied in abreactive constructs. Once defused, these revivifications can be converted to ordinary memories that are controllable, not autonomous.

Abreaction pictures often parallel the memory retrieval and working-through phases in psychotherapy. However, these images may occur at any point in the course of treatment. Prior to diagnosis they can alert the therapist to the undisclosed trauma; during treatment they are often precursors of information about to surface into consciousness. Following verbal processing in psychotherapy, abreaction pictures may serve as vehicles for ongoing working-through of newly apprehended information.

More than any other category in this ten category model, abreaction pictures can be used to tell without talking; they frequently contain long-hidden pieces of the biographical and therapeutic puzzle. Sometimes these discoveries and divulgences are too significant or portentous to be tolerated by the patient, provoking switching to another part of self.

what is this supposed

to be?

me

Switching Pictures
The Serial Self

Sometimes people are "just not themselves" and other times they "feel like a new person"; occasionally they are "beside themselves" with grief or "out of their minds" with anger. These mental states usually result from the impact of significantly charged sensory or emotional stimuli. With this in mind, one realizes that when common moodiness is combined with the varied roles people play in life and the multifaceted attributes of their personalities, the average person is very complex indeed.

As we have discussed thus far, trauma in early childhood has a distinct and significant effect on the self and its presentation in adult life. Identity, which most people take for granted, becomes an amorphous and fugitive concept for the severely abused person. Although philosophers, psychologists, and others continue to debate the complexities of identity and the self, at the simplest level identity has to do with being oneself (and not someone else) consistently under a variety of conditions. Impersonators who perform on stage or screen as if they are others are, after all, always known to be who they are, even while "being" or sounding like someone else. Those with DID do not have this flexibility or choice.

Putnam (1991), drawing upon reported observations of normal infants, has hypothesized that the changes or "switches" that occur in the adult patient with multiple personality disorder have their origin in the discontinuous state switches that occur normally during infancy. Possibly early life traumata block neurological integration of these discontinuous states of consciousness. The more the child invokes his natural capacity to dissociate during trauma, the more "practice" each state gains while in executive control of the child's mind and body. One can readily appreciate the parallel between this formulation and the concept of covert and overt ego states proposed by Watkins and Watkins (1993).

Ego states can be simply described as crystallized aspects or states of mind that comprise an internal "family of self" (Watkins & Watkins, 1993). Difficulties arise when the amnestic barriers of severe post-traumatic dissociation impede the flow of information among these fragments of self. As more and more experiences and information are gathered into these centers of control (Crabtree, 1992), the inability to access them by choice becomes increasingly problematic. Further, a state-dependent learning model suggests that effective retrieval of traumatic material requires cueing that is essentially isomorphic in nature (Spiegel, 1990). When environmental or internal cues resonate with or trigger responses from within the divided self, the dissociative person's locus of control may shift from one part of self to another. This, of course, is a broad simplification of a complex neurophysiological process that is still not well understood.

The shifting of executive control among dissociated parts or alter personalities in combination with post-traumatic amnesia sets the stage for the external dangers characterized by Kluft as the "sitting duck syndrome" (1990), as well as the vulnerability to internal threats described in Chapter 7. One can readily appreciate the hazards of a mental shift to a child state while driving on a congested highway or during physical intimacy. But even ordinary events may be disrupted by switching; for instance, switching to a socially rigid adult part with a limited behavioral or expressive repertoire while throwing a birthday party for preschoolers poses its own challenges. For the obese client, a part-self with an inability to eat may provide a temporary benefit, but ultimately one must pay the piper; switching (especially among a sizable cast of internal characters) typically creates more problems than it could ever solve. Putnam (1989) describes specific factors that increase the ability to attain control over switching. Such progress is primarily the result of acceptance of the diagnosis, along with enhanced communication and cooperation within the personality system.

There are as many metaphors for the changing of executive control within a person who has dissociative identity disorder as there are persons with the disorder. Two of the most effective ones have been described by Beahrs (1982) and Keyes (1981); the former described an orchestra coordinated by a conductor, while the latter described an internal spotlight into which alters must step for recognition or control.

While people with DID often make pictures in their various alternate personalities that are distinctive stylistically, thematically, or developmentally (Fuhrman, 1988), making these shifts within a single picture as opposed to changing from one picture to the next constitutes the uniqueness of DID art. No other psychiatric population is capable of making these kinds of graphic productions; it's that simple. Like switching phenomena in general, creation of switching pictures is the single most significant sign of this disorder evidenced in art.

Switching pictures are the pictorial equivalent of changes in handwriting seen in persons with DID (Yank, 1991). Drawings, like handwriting, are the isomorphic imprint of a person's inner dynamics at the moment; drawings and handwriting can be almost as personal and unique as fingerprints. What makes switching pictures so extraordinary is that they record the change process among parts of self, leaving behind a souvenir. These visual documents can provide graphic "proof" to DID clients, who chronically experience crises regarding the veracity of their histories and diagnoses. A switching picture can also provide a Rosetta stone for the various stylistic and developmental characteristics of graphic expressions by different parts of self. Once externalized in this way, the different internal parts can communicate with each other (and the therapist) by making pictures.

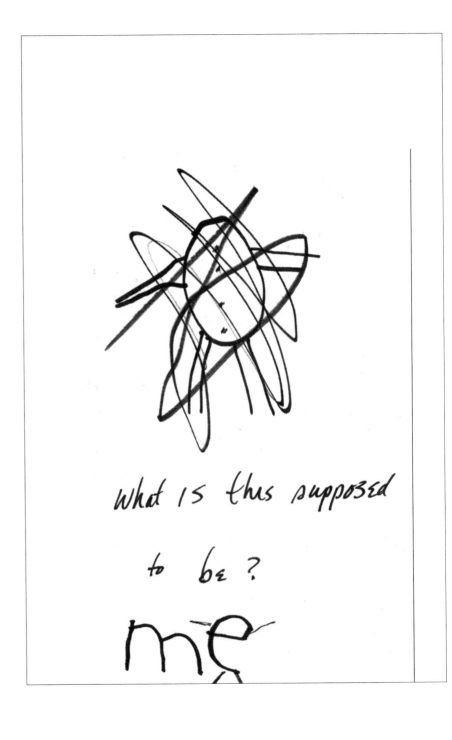

what is this supposed

to be?

me

FIGURE 11-1   **Structure:** In this picture drawn in black marker, a rudimentary headless figure floating above the center of the page has been scribbled over. Below the figure a question is written in a combination of printing and cursive handwriting; below the question, the word "me" is shakily printed, the letter "e" surrounded by four lines. The bold and simple execution is typical of the elemental style.

Meaning: The central visual focus of this drawing is the boldly scribbled-over figure. Despite having no head, hands, or feet, there are buttons down its trunk. The question posed in a rather elegant hand "what is this supposed to be?" refers back to the incomplete figure, and possibly explains its obliteration by the marks. The intense pressure and movement evident in the scribbles belie strong affect regarding the figure depicted. "Me" becomes anthropomorphized by the arms and legs attached to the letter "e," its loop suggesting a head and its curve providing a body. Thus identified, the dialogue within this drawing becomes apparent. As indicated by the level of graphic development, the figure was drawn by a young alter of a DID client. A switch between alters most likely occurred in the course of scribbling, as indicated by the change in the pressure and fluidity of the scribble. The thinner line of the scribble is congruent with the quality of handwriting below it. "Me" is the reply by the young alter who initiated the picture. To the unsuspecting observer, the meaning of this image is obscure until the link with the alter personalities is understood. The dialogue, once recognized, clarifies all levels of meaning in this drawing. The patient who drew this picture later described the "me" part of herself as "a non-functioning alter who can't move, speak, or do a whole lot."

CHAPTER 11

FIGURE 11-2

Structure: Two gestalts are placed inches apart against the white ground of the page in this marker drawing. Just above the center of the page is a small circle atop a larger circle. Randomly configured lines move this way and that across the image. All lines are drawn in black. In the lower left corner of the page stands a young girl. Black dots emanate from her eyes and red dots from her hands. A biomorphic shape is drawn in red at her feet. A single mark shaped like the letter "c" floats near the upper right corner of the page. One can see the attempt at naturalism in the figure of the girl, which, juxtaposed with the starkly elemental style of the upper form, creates a visual tension.

Meaning: The scribbled-out image at the top of the page was probably drawn first. It was apparently an attempt at a figure, hence its snowman-like quality. In this case, the developmentally young schema is covered over, most likely in favor of a more sophisticated one. This type of response is commonly seen in art by people who are reluctant to divulge their multiplicity or who are ashamed of pictures made by their younger alters. Such productions are deemed incorrect or embarrassing because they do not fit with the client's perfectionism; even if valued as an internal part, a younger alter may produce an image at a level of graphic development that seems inadequate to the adult client.

As in so many pictures by traumatized individuals, crying and bleeding are frequently drawn to externalize physical and psychological pain. The lack of mouth denotes the need for silence. Even if we did not know this picture was drawn by a survivor of childhood abuse, the graphic clues in the picture would reveal a shifting between states of consciousness, exemplified by the differing styles and levels of graphic development.

FIGURE 11-3 **Structure:** A multitude of images is depicted in a scene that includes a large and small building drawn in red with bushes flanking the doorways. In front of each door extend two rows of flowers (yellow on the right, orange on the left). A green bush sits between the house on the left and a tree. Above the tree is a yellow sun enclosed by a sawtooth yellow circle. There are three simple bird schemas above the houses. In the upper right, a horse and rider float above a swing set, on which sits a small figure, its arms outstretched. Large black zigzag lines are drawn across the page, creating visual complexity and partially obscuring the picture. Dimensionality is suggested by the converging lines of flowers, reflecting the artist's attempt to use perspective and a naturalistic style.

Meaning: At first glance, this seems to be a drawing that has been rejected by its maker, since it has been scribbled over. Looking through to the landscape image beneath, one notices a coherent composition organized along a groundline on the left, while the subjects on the right of the page seem to float; this indicates a disparity of some sort in the artist's execution of the picture. Other curious features are the facelessness of the figures, as well as the ambiguity in the relationship between the two buildings. Are they two parts of a single house, two separate houses, or are they attached? Perhaps these are symbolic self-portraits, connoting older and younger parts. It is easy to see that an ostensibly simple narrative image becomes increasingly ambiguous in its communicated meaning once certain phenomenological aspects of the picture-making are considered. The hallmark elements of a switching picture are less overt in this drawing than in many of the others in this chapter. Subtleties such as these, however, are essential for clinicians to notice if they wish to utilize art productions more effectively when they are brought into the context of therapy.

CHAPTER 11

FIGURE 11-4

Structure: Two images are drawn side by side in black marker. The popular cartoon character, Garfield, is rendered next to an incomprehensible configuration. There is no spatial or environmental context for these figures. The cartoon cat is drawn in an elemental style, featuring flatness and iconographic simplicity. It is juxtaposed on the page with its counterpart, an expressionistically drawn creature nearly abstract in nature, due to extreme distortion of form.

Meaning: It is safe to assume that the Garfield character has been copied or drawn by rote. Had this drawing been found lying on the art room table a decade ago, it would have appeared to be the result of a collaboration between two individuals, functioning at opposite ends of the cognitive continuum. Inadequate integration of form and random disorganized lines in the figure on the right are sharply contrasted with the sure, integrated cartoon schema on the left. There are subtle indications that the figure to the right is an attempt to replicate the Garfield image; however, something is seriously amiss. These two distinct portrayals of the same image probably represent concretizations of this patient's shifting mental states. The defended, smiling persona is set against the wildly distorted and disintegrated affective state. To explore meaning further in this drawing would require establishing authorship; an interview with the artist might elucidate the pictorial content. Dissociative amnesia in this case proved to be an obstacle for the artist. Not only was she unable to explain this drawing, but she did not recall making it. This level of amnesia was not typical for her, but it is relatively common for others. Thus, the meaning of this picture remains highly ambiguous.

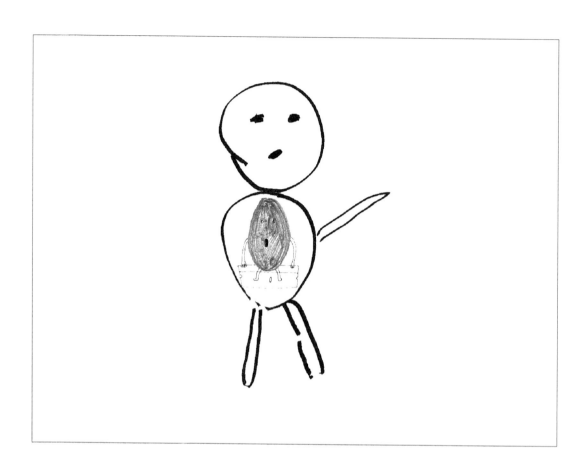

CHAPTER 11

FIGURE 11-5   **Structure:** A red oval figure atop a razor blade is seen within the torso of a boldly drawn and incomplete figure in black. The line connections in the large black figure are noticeably irregular. There is no background in this picture. Elemental style is established here through flatness and simplicity.

Meaning: Structural as well as thematic tension is the focus of this image. The use of red and black and the placement of one figure within another establish visual tension, while the screaming red face pressing down on the razor blade in proximity to the genital area creates narrative tension. Further dichotomy is conveyed in the disparity between levels of graphic development in the drawing of the two figures. The outer figure is crude, disconnected, and reflects an early level of graphic development, while the inner image is finely drawn and comparatively advanced. Created by a woman diagnosed with MPD, this seemingly obscure and confusing communication is actually quite clear. The malicious (red) alter embodies strong affect as well as self-injurious intent. Self-mutilation of various types, including cutting or other harm to the genitals, is not an uncommon behavior among survivors of severe sexual abuse. These actions, while often deeply meaningful to the client, are associated with shame and an awareness of danger if they are revealed (Miller, 1994; Ross, 1989). While disclosure of genital self-mutilation is difficult and cannot be detected without questioning by the therapist, the clues given in the art are invaluable in helping client and therapist begin to bring the behavior pattern into the treatment.

FIGURE 11-6

Structure: Various abstract shapes and crudely rendered images, drawn in charcoal, float against a field of white. In the upper left corner, a representational narrative is attempted. In the righthand corner of this boxed-in section of the picture, tiny, pale lines form an abstract design. Pressure in this segment of the picture is lighter than elsewhere on the page. One type of juxtaposition is evidenced in this way. A variety of idiosyncratic images, many with jagged edges, drawn in another style, are incorporated into this random composition.

Meaning: Loosely associated visual images convey a sense of psychosis in this rather surreal picture. Graphically, however, the inconsistency extends beyond the poorly associated and impoverished subject matter; the images inside the barrier that surround the lower right of the picture are also inconsistent in their level of graphic development from the images on the rest of the page. All of these differences reflect the subtle switches among personality states in this drawing by a young woman with DID.

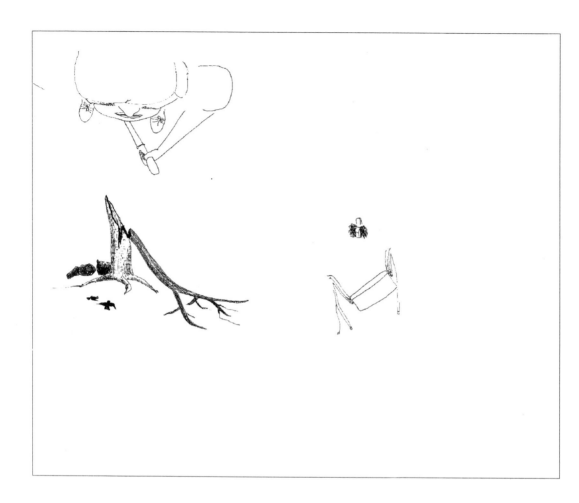

FIGURE 11-7 **Structure:** A dead bird lies beside a broken tree; at the top of the page
a girl stabs herself, as viewed from above her head; in the lower right corner,
fragments of two figures carry a rectangular container; a tiny, indistinct image
is carefully drawn above. There are no contextual references to orient these
images. Skillfully drawn in pen and ink, the images on the left of this picture
are rendered in different styles. Light and shade combined with overlapping
of images create dimensionality in the naturalistically drawn tree. The
unexpected perspective in the drawing of the girl distorts her shape and sets a
surrealist tone. On the right side of the page, the simplicity and iconographic
generalization of the figures carrying the box are typical of an elemental style.
Meaning: On first viewing, one is struck by the generally accomplished
nature of the drawing. However, there are few structural clues to lead the
viewer to a narrative comprehension of this picture's message. Thematically,
death and injury are the featured concepts of this compositionally disjointed
drawing. The ego strength necessary to render these obliquely related subjects
in this manner precludes the possibility of psychosis, except in cases of
artistically trained patients. This individual had no artistic training, which
is critical to bear in mind when seeing the complex and unusual perspectives
she employs, as exemplified by the aerial vantage of the girl. This out-of-body
view is one distinguishing factor for the identification of dissociative phenomena in this otherwise mysterious work of art, as reports of out-of-body
experiences are common in patients with multiple personality disorder.
Further, changes in style indicate the possibility of switching among different
alters. Although certain aspects of meaning in this picture are evident, the
overall meaning of the picture is considered ambiguous. The images on the
right of the page, particularly, require additional exploration.

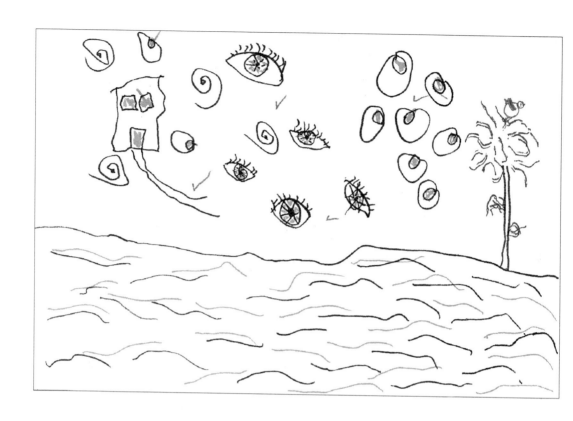

FIGURE 11-8 **Structure:** Black and yellow eyes, spirals, idiosyncratic designs, and a house float randomly above a horizontal ground of wavy black and yellow lines. A grey bird is perched atop a green and brown tree, which is connected to the groundline. Grey V-shaped marks are scattered throughout. Flatness, simplicity, stereotypy, and repetition reflect an elemental style, whereas the irrational scale, juxtaposition, and placement of the images in the upper part of the page typify surrealism. Movement is suggested by the undulating lines in the lower half of the page, as well as the floating objects above the midline. The tree and bird are drawn with surety, and their relative scale and colors are appropriate. Additionally, a more advanced graphic development is reflected in the tree's connection to the groundline.

Meaning: Poor form in the house schema and eyes, combined with the perseveration of eyes, spirals, and idiosyncratic designs, immediately suggests the possibility of neurological impairment (Bender, 1952). The idiosyncratic nature of this drawing, highlighting disconnection, exaggeration in scale, and lack of thematic integrity leads the observer to consider psychosis. Movement implied in the lower page makes it difficult to identify either landscape or water, and further suggests anxiety and instability. Keeping in mind the fact that the artist is a woman in her early forties, both options should be further explored. The inclusion of the bird and tree, however, enables the careful observer to distinguish the switch to a different level of graphic ability. One might assume that this picture, drawn by an adult diagnosed with DID, is by a young child alter until the switch is noticed on the far right of the page. This dilemma exemplifies the need for training regarding differential diagnosis through art and stages of normative graphic development when working with the art productions of individuals with DID.

FIGURE 11-9

Structure: Five separate subjects are arbitrarily placed across the page; one is drawn in pencil, the others in black and red marker. A red sun hovers above an elementally drawn house, with a figure inside the attic. A figure, loosely drawn in curlicue lines, floats in the lower right of the page. Five figures flank a curving line of red in the center of the page. In the lower left quadrant, layers of graphite suggest the form of a house, telephone pole, and sky. A tiny figure reclines atop a giant knife in the upper left of the page. Overall, elementalism is utilized in the four subjects drawn in marker; each is flat and distilled to its simplest essence. The unexpected juxtaposition of the tiny figure, surprisingly paired with the large knife, is surrealistic. The handling of the pencil work in the scene at the lower left suggests movement and is executed in an expressionistic manner.

Meaning: At first glance, one is struck by the unrelated imagery, compositional disconnection, and stylistic disparity within this picture. It would seem that several people have drawn on this page serially but not in a collaborative fashion. There is no focal point; each section draws attention to itself. This picture was, in fact, drawn by one woman. Its stylistic and developmental inconsistencies are hallmarks of the switching picture.

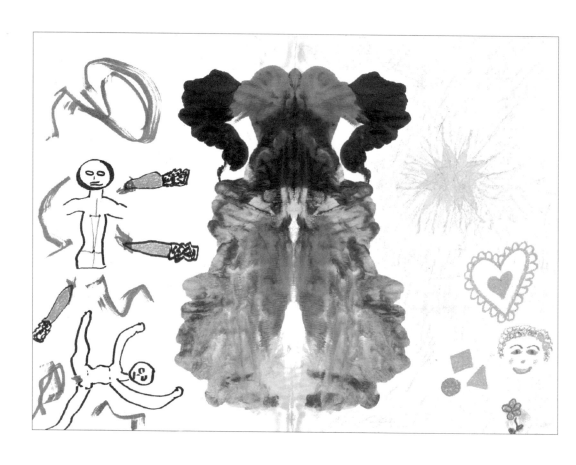

FIGURE 11-10

Structure: Divided into three vertical sections, this composition juxtaposes media as well as images and styles. The section on the left, drawn in black and red marker, features two naked figures. The upper figure is only a head and torso, the lower a supine female figure, her arms and legs extended. Three red-tipped knives point toward the upper figure; they float in space. The negative space is marked with red scribbles. The central section is a "blot" made from red, blue, and yellow paints. Its form is bold, fluid, symmetrical, and biomorphic. The right section of the page is dominated by a yellow star-like form, radiating outward. In the lower right corner, a pink heart, a woman's face, a red flower, and green, pink, and blue geometric shapes are randomly placed. The picture is primarily expressionistic, due to the distortion of form, saturated polychrome, and implied movement; however, the items in the lower right corner are drawn in the elemental style.

Meaning: The distinctive styles and different affective tones of the images here convey the impression of a group endeavor, as if this piece was a group mural. The violent content on the left juxtaposed with the cheerful imagery on the right might also suggest psychosis. However, to the informed viewer the disparity in graphic styles and content suggests multiplicity. The image in the center of the page (although unintentional) strongly resembles a headless figure, its arms akimbo; its pelvic area oozes red. This element functions like a barrier between the menacing imagery on the left and the stereotypic content on the right. In this instance, media and mood changed along with switches among personalities.

FIGURE 11-11 **Structure:** A variety of styles, colors, and levels of graphic development comprises this composition of randomly placed figures and images. Exaggeration allows the bottle at the right to be the same scale as the stick figure below it to the left and the tree directly above it. At the center of the picture are multicolored shapes drawn expressionistically due primarily to the limitations of early developmental graphic ability. This is in marked contrast to the finely drawn and highly embellished design in the lower left corner of the page. All four human figures are done in the elemental style, with two additional characters suggested merely by the inclusion of two pairs of eyes (inside the tree and inside the box at the upper right). Surrealism, although a minor characteristic of this picture, is seen in the unexpected placement of the face inside the tree. There is also writing in the picture.

Meaning: It is almost impossible to "break the code" of this drawing, due to its personal, idiosyncratic nature. The clinician familiar with normative stages of graphic development will quickly recognize the apparent inconsistencies. Changes in style as well as levels of graphic development are hallmarks of switching in the art of people with DID. These are not seen in the art of nondissociative psychotics or in art of other psychiatric patients. Here one sees a rare but important example of serial switching among a "family" of alters of a single patient on the same page. The clinician must take pains to be aware of the various schemas in the ongoing art productions of each client in order to read the clues these images convey. Observant readers may have noticed a familiar character from a previous illustration drawn by the same client, Figure 11-1, located in the upper left corner of this page. Each image on this page represents either an alter within the system or a concept important to one of the alters.

Conclusion   Because there is no central agent controlling the overall creation of switching pictures, these compositions frequently exhibit randomness and juxtaposition. Juxtaposition in switching pictures happens as different drawing styles are combined within the same drawing. In contrast to drawings in other categories, images do not seem to be juxtaposed for the purpose of comparison; nor do they always appear to be placed in proximity to suggest unspoken relationships. Boldness is typically seen when one alter personality emerges to negate a previously drawn image or to add some marks to the page. Randomness in these pictures is probably the result of indiscriminate placement of elements, perhaps resulting from disorientation caused by rapidly shifting states of consciousness.

Typically, switches are represented in one of several ways: scribbling over or crossing out images; side-by-side placement of dissimilar styles and levels of graphic development; and crumpling, tearing-up, or throwing away pictures. None of these methods of obliterating images, in and of itself, constitutes switching behavior. The former two phenomena, however, are more conspicuous because they allow the product to survive the process. The latter set of behaviors may be executed in a dramatic or surreptitious fashion and may have nothing whatsoever to do with the process of switching.

Schaverien explains the disposal of artwork by clients in treatment through what she calls the "scapegoat transference," "where the picture is being blamed for the deed, or the material it reveals" (1992, p. 50). Thus the undesirable material, once externalized, can be split off and banished, allowing that which is acceptable to be held (unseen) within. She also points out the futility of "killing the messenger," since the picture's disposal only delays the "inevitable conscious realization of the message which it bears" (p. 51).

Recognizing differences in levels of graphic development is crucial to detecting switching pictures. For information on these levels the reader is directed to the writings of Lowenfeld and Brittain (1987), Cox (1992), Golomb (1992), and Rubin (1978). It is important to remember that, because of the multileveled nature of artwork, there is always a danger in making judgments about pictures and their messages, especially without conferring with their creators. The switching picture's original function and message may be subverted by the shift. Sometimes, however, a switch can be illuminating. To understand the dynamics of the process, one must notice where in the

System Pictures

FIGURE 3-3

(See page 26.)

FIGURE 3-10

(See page 37.)

Chaos Pictures

FIGURE 4-5   (See page 51.)

FIGURE 4-8   (See page 55.)

Fragmentation Picture

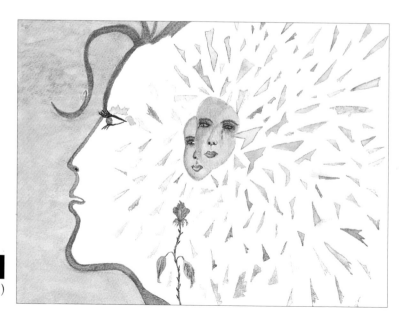

FIGURE 5-4

(See page 68.)

Barrier Pictures

FIGURE 6-12s-a (See page 103.)

FIGURE 6-12s-b (See page 103.)

FIGURE 6-12s-c (See page 103.)

FIGURE 6-12s-d (See page 103.)

Threat Pictures

FIGURE 7-1
(See page 109.)

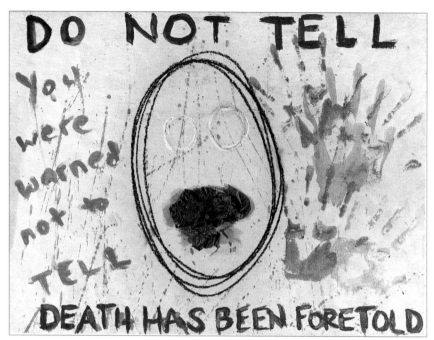

FIGURE 7-5   (See page 115.)

Induction Pictures

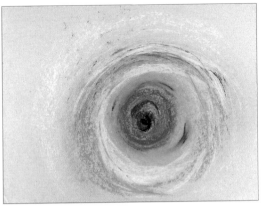

FIGURE 8-9 (See page 138.)

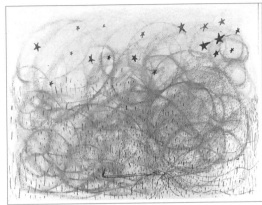

FIGURE 8-11 (See page 141.)

Trance Pictures

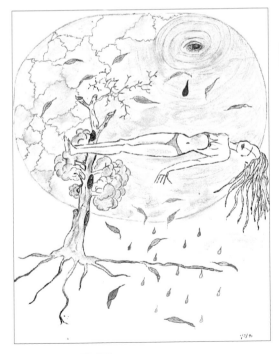

FIGURE 9-2 (See page 149.)

FIGURE 9-8 (See page 159.)

Abreaction
Pictures

FIGURE 10-3

(See page 175.)

FIGURE 10-10a

(See page 189.)

Switching Pictures

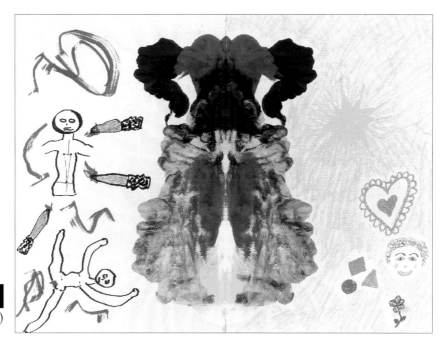

FIGURE 11-10
(See page 215.)

FIGURE 11-11
(See page 217.)

Alert
Pictures

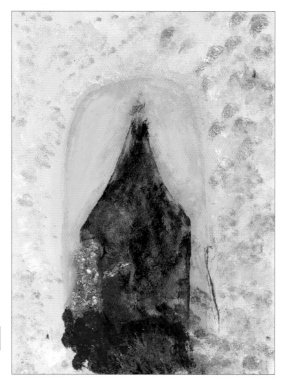

FIGURE 12-1

(See page 225.)

FIGURE 13-10b

(See page 285.)

picture the switch occurs and how it is manifested.

Switching pictures may increase in frequency during periods of heightened stress brought on by anniversary dates of significant traumas or current life events experienced as overwhelming. For the pre-diagnosis DID patient, throwing pictures away may be the most effective way to hide any potential clues regarding abuse, dissociation, or multiplicity. For the DID patient in the midst of therapy, scribbling over and crossing out images might indicate a struggle between what has traditionally been referred to as the "host personali-ty" (the part of self that is "out" for the longest periods of time) and the other alters or parts of self. These struggles typically involve issues of acceptance regarding diagnosis, willingness to allow externalization of multiplicity (Figure 11-1), and ability to tolerate disclosure of abuse experiences. When these issues become less problematic—although they frequently remain of some concern throughout the course of treatment—coexistence of different drawing styles and distinctive personality representations may be more tolerable (Figure 11-10). In any case, the frequency of switching pictures varies in relation to changing dynamics within and outside the treatment frame.

Looking at the drawings that can be readily identified as switching pictures, we detect no obvious rule of thumb concerning the clarity of meaning. Some of these creations appear to have been made as joint efforts by more than one person (Figure 11-4) and, if accepted as such, their meaning would be relatively clear. When images are crossed out (e.g., Figure 11-2), it looks as if someone had simply changed his or her mind midway through the process; no further detective work seems necessary. More complex pictures, which include a variety of styles and strategies (e.g., Figures 11-9, 11-10), are more likely to be experienced as highly ambiguous or obscure due to their arcane content and compositions, reminiscent of trance pictures.

An awareness of the possibility of switching in art has enormous implications for diagnosis and treatment. The switching picture functions as the quintessential note of alert to the presence of dissociative identity in the client-artist. However, not all people are willing or able to communicate their secrets of a lifetime either to themselves or their therapists in this manner; consciously or not, they adopt other ways of making art to profit from its inherent multileveledness.

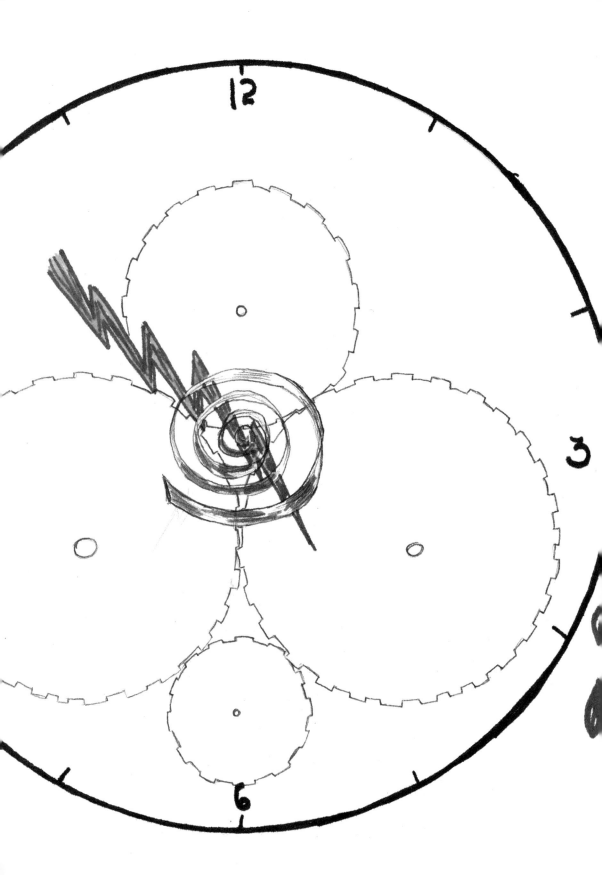

Chapter 12

Alert Pictures
Telling Without Talking

The sheer number of secrets that accumulates within the lifetime of a person with DID is noteworthy. Beginning with the initial violation by an abuser, nearly everything of significance in her life and many inconsequential things as well is added to the confidences and betrayals she must protect in order to maintain her own sense of safety (Herman, 1992). According to Putnam, "Secrets have a power of their own that pressures the patient both to conceal and to reveal them" (1989, p. 175). Even upon entering psychotherapy, the survivor of severe, chronic childhood trauma might defend her earliest (or most recent) secret to the best of her ability.

Since the perpetrator often suggests to the young victim that what is actually happening is only a figment of her imagination, subsequent recall of the event can be fraught with disbelief. The child's initial attempt at disclosure typically goes unheeded (Courtois, 1988), reinforcing suppression of the truth. Once multiplicity develops (prior to adolescence) the patient-to-be becomes engaged in a hide-and-seek game with herself concerning the state of her own unity. It is not uncommon for a person to be "unaware" of her own multiplicity until well into adulthood (Ross, 1989). The majority of dissociative people maintain their conditions in utmost silence (Kluft, 1985), even hiding from their partners and therapists (Gelinas, 1983). Patients with DID often remain in abusive situations even after extensive treatment, fiercely withholding the evidence. Inevitably, many of these patients enter therapy with clinicians who do not themselves acknowledge the existence of the disorder, denying the patient an opportunity for affirmation. Thus, the cycle of secrecy continues in the adult survivor of childhood abuse.

Each new equivocation adds another corridor to the byzantine maze in the mind and life of the survivor of severe childhood trauma. Dissociative post-traumatic amnesia complicates this matter; as substantial gaps in memory develop for autobiographical experiences and BASK levels become isolated from one another, amnestic barriers become increasingly more prominent in the thought process.

Being told "not to know"; "it couldn't possibly have happened—why would you make up such a thing?"; "there's nothing wrong with you, get on with your life"; "our family members are the only ones who care about you"; and "I'm sorry, but you must stop trying to prove that there's something special about your history," continually reinforces the patient's difficulties in assessing what is real and what is not. Consequently, she remains trapped in her maze of confusion, shame, and self-doubt.

The person's need to reveal and to conceal creates a dilemma that is not easily addressed in verbal psychotherapy. Since the inherent multileveledness of art provides an effective vehicle for the simultaneous revealing and concealing of information (Cohen & Cox, 1989), art is the most efficient way for people with severe dissociative conditions to externalize their conflicts and inner worlds (Cohen, in press).

Brainwashing of child victims of abuse takes place within a "climate of pervasive terror" (Herman, 1992, p. 98), in which control is maintained by verbal threats of death to the victim and others. Fortunately, it is the rare offender who forbids making art about his transgressions; typically the threats are to "not tell." Even more fortunately for these clients, art gives them the opportunity to maintain their primal oaths and still tell their stories without talking.

Alert pictures function like "SOS" signals from a ship in peril. They are typically coded compositions that range from the completely innocuous to the utterly inscrutable. In between, one sees imagery that attracts the viewer's attention but does not easily divulge its secrets. Coding that results from extreme stylization of form in these types of pictures usually serves to cover up sexually explicit and violent material, as well as references to multiplicity. Some alert pictures reflect intense affect, while others are cold and mechanistic in appearance. The crucial factor in recognizing alert pictures is that each one seems to say, "Look at this . . . ," and when one begins to look carefully, the message changes to "Why are you looking at this?" This is an important lesson about looking at psychiatric art: pictures that are equivocal in their manifest messages often have the most startling information to share.

FIGURE 12-1 **Structure:** Saturated color is the predominant feature of this painting on paper. A rich arch of bright yellow surrounds a murky black central area. Dark red encloses this shape at its base. Just above it, to the left, one notices amorphous and indistinct passages of silver and blue. Set against a pale yellow background, the entire image is surrounded by a dappled random pattern of black, grey, and white. This implied movement, coupled with the intense colors employed, is reminiscent of the expressionist style.

Meaning: An air of mystery surrounds this highly ambiguous painting, diffuse in its mottled surface and sculptural in its boldly shaped colors. The viewer is upended at every visual turn. At first glance, one might see brightly colored drapery framing a darkened picture window. After more scrutiny, a faceless head with blond hair appears. The blood red area at the bottom of the page, however, remains troubling and at odds with the aforementioned themes. At this point, the image of a woman bent over at the waist (seen from behind) might come to the fore. This is the kind of interplay between revealing and concealing one might expect to see in the artwork of people with DID. (Figure 10-7 was done by the same client at a point when she was revealing rather than concealing the story of her abuse.)

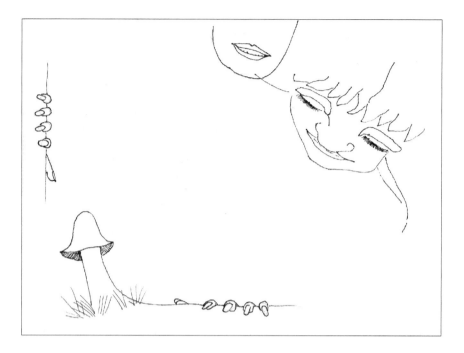

FIGURE 12-2

Structure: The images that are central to this surreal line drawing are placed peripherally on the page; the center itself is blank. A naturalistically drawn mushroom is surrounded by grass. To the right, coming over the groundline, are five pointed fingernails. This image is repeated along the upper left side of the page. In the upper right corner are two disembodied heads. The head on the left is simply a face's outline with a smiling mouth. The other is a young girl's head, viewed from an aerial perspective.

Meaning: The sexual content of the picture is barely disguised due to the overtly phallic quality of the mushroom. A sense of malevolence and disconnection also pervades the composition. The claw-like fingers provide the key to unlocking the mystery of this surreal juxtaposition of images. Once the groundline is recognized as an abdomen and the grass as pubic hair, then the girl's head hovering above the penis/mushroom can be understood in the context of fellatio. The mouth on the face to the left further supports the notion of dissociation from the physical act, itself an out-of-body experience.

FIGURE 12-3

Structure: A solid circle is boldly painted in black inside a larger circle. Above it, scribbled lines form an irregular wedge shape. Below it, two irregular vertical lines are drawn. The words "me now" are written to the right of the image.

Meaning: A crudely drawn figure, its head a giant eye topped with a mass of hair, is precariously placed on fragile stilt-like legs. "Me now" may refer to this simple self-portrait. The irregular line quality coupled with the elementalism of form and disjointed lettering might indicate neurological impairment in an adult client (Bender, 1952). However, the woman who drew this picture did not have such a disorder, as other examples of her work will illustrate (Figures 3-7a, 4-7). In fact, "me" refers to an alter personality who "took over," according to the client, when she was raped; that is the purpose of this personality. The viewer might also notice that the configuration could depict a penis adjacent to a tuft of pubic hair. The artist stated, "We would think we would turn into the object," indicating the lack of ego boundaries during this altered state of consciousness. The multileveled nature of artmaking allows for the simultaneous coding of this self-portrait as person and penis.

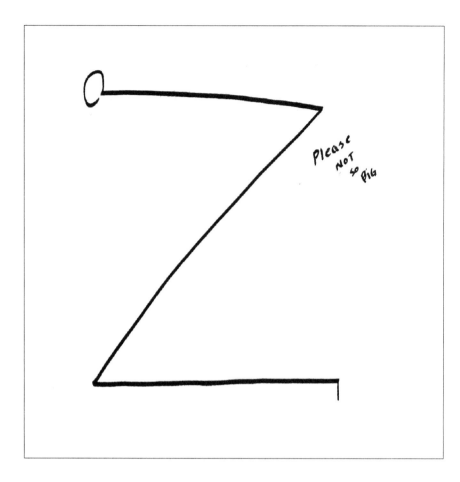

CHAPTER 12

FIGURE 12-4

Structure: A bold and simply drawn design in the shape of the letter Z is minimally enhanced by a loop at its top and a small vertical line at its bottom. Although there is no environmental context for this singular image, the words "please not so big" are penned in small letters at the upper right of the drawing.

Meaning: Images as simple as this one give the observer few clues to their intended meaning. In this case the words lend little help, and might be interpreted as the idiosyncratic musings of an individual with a thought disorder. Does the letter Z have any special significance to the maker? What importance do the small embellishments have in this configuration? Until one recognizes the highly stylized kneeling figure with its circular head and downward pointing foot, it is difficult to ascertain the intended communication of the artist.

Alert pictures, as illustrated by this highly coded drawing, provide the client with the opportunity to simultaneously reveal and conceal to varying extents, depending on their own conscious awareness of their history, diagnosis, and willingness to disclose to the therapist. This picture reflects the intense ambivalence around communicating a scenario in which the patient, as a child, was anally raped by an adult perpetrator. According to the artist, the Z-shaped figure represents a "zippermouth" alter who was not allowed to talk about the abuse.

CHAPTER 12

FIGURE 12-5   **Structure:** A pencil drawing naturalistically depicts a suspended cylindrical object surrounded by a ring. Tiny droplets fall from its tip into a spiraling design. Within several drops and near the bottom of the page are minuscule stick figures. The lack of embellishments in the background results in a simple image.

Meaning: There is no escaping a sexual reading of this picture, in which a phallic form penetrates a circular opening. The expelled droplets reinforce this interpretation. The spiraling pool suggests trance induction. It is interesting to note that the tiny stick figures, which might otherwise communicate "making babies," refer in this instance to the development of dissociated part-selves, according to the woman who drew it. The mechanical look of the coitus is indicative of her detached response to the repetitive rape experience. Although the somewhat overt content of this drawing might alert the therapist to the sexual communication of the client, the theme of multiplicity might be overlooked.

CHAPTER 12

FIGURE 12-6

Structure: Drawn in colored pencil against a background of light red, a dark hourglass shape is at the center bottom of the picture. Crowded across the top of the page are 31 circles, each with a pair of eyes and eyebrows colored in red, yellow, and blue. A successive pattern of curved lines continues down toward the center of the page, and in each sequential row the lines flatten until they overlap with the top of the hourglass shape.

Meaning: Unless the viewer has a context for this image, interpretation is difficult. The only recognizable content is the group of mouthless faces across the top of the page. The perseverative lines beneath them suggest some sort of transformation as they progressively change shape. The hourglass configuration is ambiguous, in that it can be read as both positive and negative form. When it is perceived as negative (the space between things), the symmetrical rounded shapes that nearly touch are emphasized. These may indicate breasts or buttocks, particularly because they are pink and flesh-toned. The dark curved wedge, seen as figure rather than ground, may be the delta of pubic hair in a woman's crotch, its darkness mingling with the shadow between the thighs beneath. In any case, most of the content options seem to be sexual.

The patterned lines originating from mid-page just above this area develop into the well-defined circle-faces as they progress up the page. The beginnings of a dissociative response are seen in the perseverative markings of induction and the formation of a system of alter personalities. The mouthlessness of these entities reflects the secrecy of the abuse. Since the affect is downplayed in this drawing due to the highly controlled use of media, light pressure, symmetrical configuration, and muted color, the viewer is given little indication of its traumatic content.

CHAPTER 12

FIGURE 12-7   **Structure:** A young girl, facing away from the viewer, stands at the end of a hall of doorways. The girl holds up the back of her dress. The drawing emphasizes deep space through the use of linear perspective and the sequential placement of the doors.

Meaning: This relatively benign image evokes a sense of isolation and loneliness and might be interpreted as an expression of depression by a psychiatric patient. At one time in this woman's life she was diagnosed as having catatonic schizophrenia. One can easily imagine the adult woman standing rigidly in the hallway of a psychiatric ward in a state institution, while inside a frightened little girl stares out. Although the figure of the girl is nearly as tall as the closest doorway, she looks to be of preschool age.

Her body is drawn in a way that suggests she is both facing the viewer and turning away. Further, by lifting her dress she is exposing her underpants, but it is not clear whether the viewer is seeing them from the front or the back. In any case, this self-exposure is the central focus of the drawing. In this way the client alludes to her victimization, while the receding doorways cleverly refer to her multiplicity. The message of such a subtle picture could be easily overlooked.

FIGURE 12-8

Structure: Angularity is contrasted with circularity in this monochromatic drawing of a tree. Naturalism is suggested through the dimensionality of the container in which the tree rests, as well as the overlapping layers of the foliage. There is no specific pattern to the placement of small round shapes, nor do the horizontal lines dividing the tree create any pattern. Surrealism is also suggested through the juxtaposition of the many tiny faces (as well as the large one) with the tree.

Meaning: Frankly unhappy Christmas imagery is uncommon. As if the frowning faces on each of the ornaments were not enough, the message of "merry fuckin christmas" on the bucket presses the message home. The large frowning face atop the tree, combined with the winding line around its girth, suggests a somewhat anthropomorphized image of bondage or restraint. This is one element distinguishing this drawing as an alert picture (referring to multiplicity), rather than as the work of a disgruntled holiday Scrooge. The young woman who drew this image infused this otherwise clichéd scene with personal meaning.

FIGURE 12-9

Structure: A full-length figure stands with arms akimbo against a hot pink background. A large heart-shaped design is placed against her chest; it encloses a scene in which several figures are depicted. The blue blouse and green skirt are flatly painted, making a bold contrast between these cool colors and the warm background. Details in the delineation of the woman's face and the heart-shaped configuration suggest an attempt at naturalistic style.

Meaning: An adult woman faces the viewer in a somewhat confrontational stance. Her demeanor appears rather stern in contrast to the intimate, playful scene inside the heart shape. Despite the matter-of-fact style of the heart, there is no way to make sense of it in relation to the woman's body. Is it a design on her blouse, a large decorative accessory, or a window into the subject's feelings about a memory she holds in her heart? In the authors' experience, the depiction of subsidiary figures within a larger figure or inside a head should alert the therapist to the possibility of multiplicity in the maker. When asked about this image, the client stated that she was painting a picture of a safe place for one of her child alter personalities.

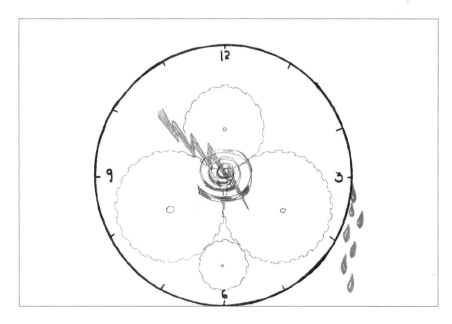

FIGURE 12-10

Structure: A clockface is boldly drawn in marker, its internal spring and gears exposed to view. A red and yellow zig-zag design is juxtaposed with the central spiral. Red droplets fall from the right side of the clock's perimeter, just below the number three. The remainder of the page is blank. The irrational juxtaposition of a lightning bolt, red droplets, and a clock denote a surrealist style.

Meaning: The choice of a clock as the central feature of this drawing allows for a variety of connotations. Time, of course, is the most obvious message, yet there are no hands on this clock. The emphasis on the inner mechanism bespeaks issues of functioning, interdependence, and tightly-wound tension. The intruding lightning bolt disturbs this equilibrium, and the dripping blood may be the result.

Both the transparency of the clock and the surreal juxtaposition of the blood might suggest the loose cognitive associations of psychotic process. However, there are several clues here to DID: DID is a disorder of time (Putnam, 1989); the meshing gears are a metaphor for the workings of a personality system; the penetrating lightning bolt portrays the impact of trauma; and dripping blood is a ubiquitous indication of physical or psychological pain. Thus the client is able to communicate a message of trauma, hurt, time loss, and multiplicity, but in a rather oblique, restrained manner.

Conclusion No single artmaking strategy or style is specific to alert pictures. Conceivably any of the four styles and any of the artmaking strategies could be used. One reason for this is the concurrent presence of "reveal and conceal" methodology; both boldness and diffusion, for instance, could be used (though skill would be required to include them in the same picture). This duality should not be confused with the different approaches seen in switching pictures, though; presumably, parts of self are overtly or covertly cooperating on alert pictures, while they might be in direct conflict when a switching picture manifests.

Alert pictures are first and foremost about content and not form. Their themes, as have been mentioned, are usually abuse or trauma, dissociation, and multiplicity. Content will include disguised representations of physical and sexual victimization at all levels of severity (Figures 12-2, 12-3), as well as bizarre and sadistic scenarios including cannibalism, bestiality, premature burial, bondage, electroshock, drowning, and human sacrifice. Often different alters will contribute their experiences of the abuse, which may result in the creation of a series of abreaction pictures related to a specific event (see Figures 13-9a through 13-9l). Dissociation and multiplicity will be represented in ways reminiscent of other categories, especially system pictures (Figure 12-5, 12-6). In any case, the restraint that distinguishes these pictures from those in related categories is due to the give-and-take between alters regarding whether to reveal, what to reveal, and how much.

The level of clarity of communication in these works depends on the stage of treatment and the extent of the client's waking consciousness during the making of the picture. Some alert pictures are frankly created as "tests" of the therapist's acumen; dissociative clients are frequently testing limits, boundaries, skills, and trustworthiness of their therapists. This helps them to establish a sense of safety (though it is constantly shifting) within the treatment. The therapist to whom these pictures are presented should keep in mind that the client is trying to tell about her life experiences and her inner truth without talking.

Chapter 13

Cara, A Case Study
Breaking the Code

The theoretical model identifying the ten categories that distinguish MPD art was developed over seven years. It is based upon analysis of approximately four thousand spontaneous pictures, as well as discussions with clients and therapists during that period. It had its origin, however, in the drawings and thoughts of one woman. A client intermittently in art therapy with each of the authors over more than a decade, Cara (a pseudonym) inspired the professional collaboration that resulted in this book.

The artwork shown was made by Cara at home, in day treatment, in outpatient adjunctive art therapy, and in psychiatric hospitals. Some pictures were created during individual art therapy sessions, others in group. They are culled from a body of greater than one thousand pictures. This chapter is offered as an example of how the ten category model manifests in the work of a client prior to diagnosis and during the course of treatment.

Brief History Cara is a 49-year-old Caucasian woman born into an upper-middle-class family, the youngest of four girls. Her father, a brilliant scientist, was also a pillar of his church community. Cara's mother was a nurse. Each of the daughters in the family has acknowledged physical abuse at the hands of the parents, and all required psychiatric care at one time or another; one sister has been diagnosed with chronic schizophrenia.

Cara's memories of abuse extend back to the time she was a toddler and include both physical and sexual victimization by her parents, extended family, and others: sadistic, physical, and sexual violence of all types, including bondage, attempted drowning, and anal and oral penetration until the age of 16. She recalls a hiatus in these activities between the ages of six and ten. Her parents performed a hymenectomy on her at the age of ten, facilitating the practice of vaginal penetrations with foreign objects, as well as rapes by her father. This behavior culminated in at least one pregnancy by the father and a subsequent abortion (performed by her mother) against Cara's will.

Cara attended college for two years. There she met a man whom she married at age 19. She continued her education to become a licensed practical nurse and practiced nursing for a year in labor and delivery. Cara has two sons, ages 22 and 26, and has recently become a grandmother. She has published poetry and short stories and enjoys photography.

The client suggests that she and her family of origin would have seemed unremarkable. In 1979, when she was 32, memories of her abuse began to surface. It was at this time that she had her first psychiatric hospitalization. Cara was initially diagnosed as having depression. Later, her diagnosis was changed to bipolar disorder (manic depression), and eventually to borderline personality disorder. In 1980 she was attending a day treatment program when Carol Cox, at that time a graduate student in art therapy, began to work with her; this relationship lasted two years since Cox was subsequently employed as the art therapist of the facility.

Rediagnosed with temporal lobe epilepsy, Cara sought consultation with another psychiatrist in 1985. At that time, her diagnosis was changed to multiple personality disorder and she was sent to the National Institute of Mental Health for diagnostic clarification. There she participated in the seminal research by Putnam and others (1986), in which electroencephalograms were administered to each of five alter personalities on separate occasions over a period of two weeks. According to Cara, distinct EEGs were recorded for each of the five; one child alter exhibited brain waves consistent with those of children. Temporal lobe epilepsy was ruled out.

Cara was hospitalized in the wake of suicide attempts on a number of occasions. All in all, she had been hospitalized eleven times before being admitted in 1987 to the community hospital in which Barry Cohen served as art therapist on the psychiatric unit. Less than a year later, the authors began to collaborate on a study of Cara's art.

Cohen worked as art therapist with Cara individually and in group both in and outside the hospital during the following three years. Although she continued to be hospitalized periodically for a variety of medical reasons, her psychiatric stays became infrequent. During the last several years multiple sclerosis began to dominate her health. At first, she was able to summon alters not affected by the multiple sclerosis; these parts were still able to express themselves through art, a pastime she dearly enjoyed; unfortunately, this did not last. By 1992, her tremors had become so severe that she was unable to draw, and was she confined to a bed and a wheelchair.

Following work with another psychiatrist, and after making some peace with her medical and mental disorders, Cara was able to integrate a substantial portion of her alter personality system, which by that time ranged in excess of 75 parts. She credits her newfound spiritual focus, her supportive family and friends, and her lifelong sense of humor as chief factors in her recovery. Very recently, she underwent neurological surgery that substantially reduced her tremors. She hopes to resume her creative work in the future.

The following pictures are described briefly, primarily due to their sheer number. The vast majority of these drawings were made with colored markers; those that were not will be indicated. The reader is encouraged to observe the parallels within each category, as well as the coded imagery that unfolded during a decade of treatment.

FIGURE 13-1a
(1980)

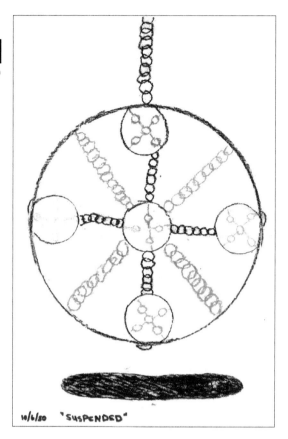

10/6/80 "SUSPENDED"

FIGURE 13-1b
(1987)

System Pictures

In 1980, five years before she was given the diagnosis of MPD (and before the intense resurgence of interest in and publications about this disorder), Cara made this picture (Figure 13-1a), which she titled "Suspended," in response to an assignment to draw a mandala. The first image of this theme drawn in treatment, it also organizes parts within a whole. Figures 13-1b and 13-1c were drawn in the late 1980s, some years after her MPD diagnosis was established. By this time, she was consciously aware of her system of alter personalities, which was comprised of families of four. In both drawings the "core symbol" is depicted as a fetal shape; in the latter, it is located in the center, and in the former at the bottom center.

FIGURE 13-1c

(1987)

During one of several hospitalizations in the late eighties, Cara found herself in the art room drawing this image of chaining boxes (Figure 13-1d). She was compelled to color them in, but refrained from allowing the colors to touch; later she noted that blending was tantamount to fusing (personalities). All at once she ceased coloring the boxes and, days afterward, realized the colored boxes totaled the number of her parts she was aware of to date. The tree image (Figure 13-1e), also drawn during that period, is a representational (though surreal) totemic system. As has been mentioned previously, trees are often used as self symbols in the artwork of MPD clients.

When Cara drew Figure 13-1f in 1980, she explained that it depicted her family at her graveside. This, of course, did not address the multicolored fetal

FIGURE 13-1d

(1987)

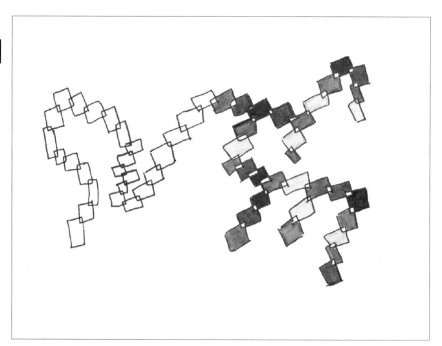

FIGURE 13-1e
(1989)

FIGURE 13-1f
(1980)

symbol from whom the thought emanates. Seven or eight years later, Figure 13-1g overtly dealt with the freakish self-concept held by many MPD clients, thus the platypus on display. The figures are again gathered to witness, just as in the earlier picture. The multicolored flower, drawn in the same space as its fetal predecessor, reflects the growth of the system in size, complexity, and metaphor. When Cara looked at Figure 13-1f recently, she said, "If Carol had asked me in 1980, I would have translated it into something socially appropriate because I think that's what multiples do. They see (what they have drawn) and they get shocked and say, 'Oh God, what can I say that is socially appropriate that won't get me in trouble?'"

FIGURE 13-1g
(1988)

FIGURE 13-1e
(1989)

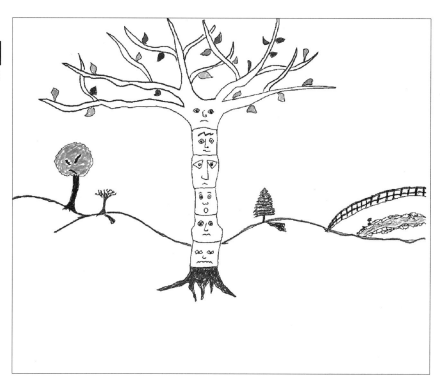

FIGURE 13-1f
(1980)

symbol from whom the thought emanates. Seven or eight years later, Figure 13-1g overtly dealt with the freakish self-concept held by many MPD clients, thus the platypus on display. The figures are again gathered to witness, just as in the earlier picture. The multicolored flower, drawn in the same space as its fetal predecessor, reflects the growth of the system in size, complexity, and metaphor. When Cara looked at Figure 13-1f recently, she said, "If Carol had asked me in 1980, I would have translated it into something socially appropriate because I think that's what multiples do. They see (what they have drawn) and they get shocked and say, 'Oh God, what can I say that is socially appropriate that won't get me in trouble?'"

FIGURE 13-1g
(1988)

Chaos Pictures

The complex image in Figure 13-2a was drawn by Cara in 1980. She did not understand what it signified, so it remained untitled until some years later. She eventually described it as a "war zone" picture, describing the extraordinary state of conflict and confusion when her system was in disarray. "War zone is almost a physical state with us . . . you just get absolutely immobilized while this goes on in your head," she stated. The tissue paper collage of red and pink (Figure 13-2b) also describes this state. Its center, the core image, is clouded over due to the chaos within. Figure 13-2b was also made in 1980, long before the notion of systems and cores was part of her vocabulary and understanding.

FIGURE 13-2a
(1980)

FIGURE 13-2b
(1980)

FIGURE 13-2c
(1988)

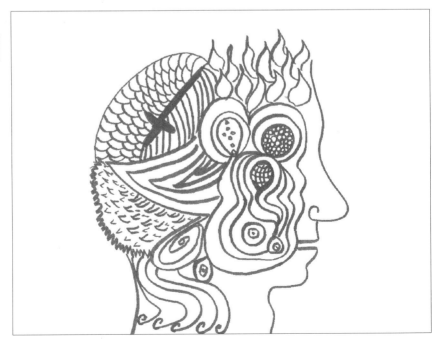

Figures 13-2c and 13-2d were drawn approximately eight years after the previous two pictures. In the first of these two images, an x-ray view reveals complex organizations of energy within the head; the front area at the top of the head seems to be aflame. In the next image, inscribed "you better get me out of this damn place," male and female figures struggle to literally free themselves from the effects of chaos by prying open their scalps. An elaborate fireworks-like display bursts forth from the crouching woman's head.

FIGURE 13-2d
(1988)

YOU BETTER
GET ME OUT OF THIS
DAMN PLACE.

FIGURE 13-3a
(1982)

FIGURE 13-3b
(1982)

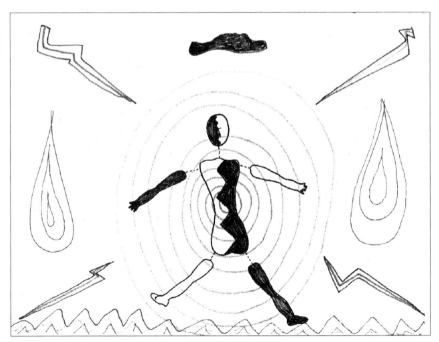

Fragmentation Pictures

At the bottom of Figure 13-3a, Cara in 1982 wrote, "to interpret I need Carol Cox." Unfortunately, Carol was out ill from work that day. The overt metaphors available to the casual onlookers were "bursting" and "cracking-up," not inconceivable to the chronically ill people who participated in day treatment. With more than a decade of hindsight, the issue of shattered identity is concretized. Inexplicably titled "Farewell," Figure 13-3b was also drawn in 1982. The disconnected figure was seen at the time to embody many of the themes associated with the artwork of borderline personality disorder (BPD) clients: the black and white split, the predominance of black and red, and the so-called suicidal spiral (Cox, 1985). Although BPD is coexistent in approximately 70% of MPD patients (Kemp, Gilbertson, & Torem, 1988), this particular composition was communicating a sense of fragmentation within the context of hypnotic trance. Similar themes are reflected in later work (Figure 13-3c), which depicts a vertically layered figure on the left, a disconnected robotic figure at the top, and a dematerializing figure at the lower right.

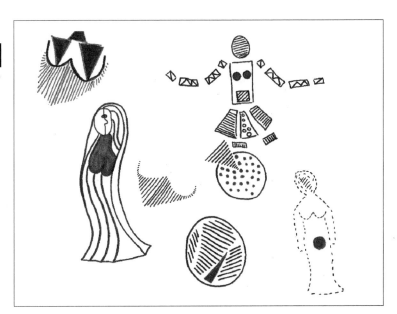

FIGURE 13-3c
(1987)

FIGURE 13-3d
(1982)

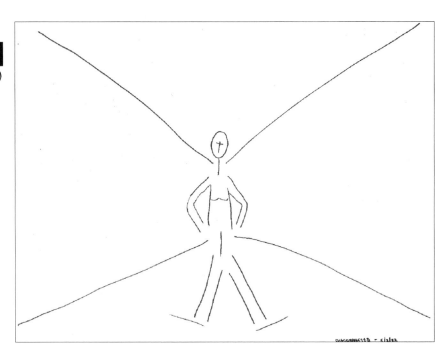

FIGURE 13-3e
(1988)

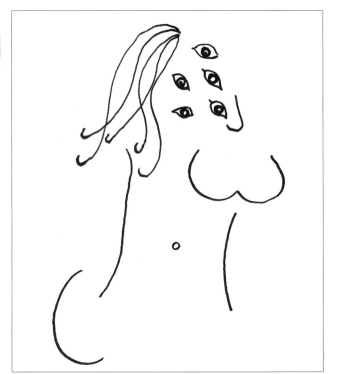

Figure 13-3d was drawn in 1982. It is a very simple evocation of the disconnected body sense in fragmentation. Notice the generic representation of the human figure in this and other pictures in this chapter. It is the safest possible schema for a self that is comprised of parts of both genders. Many years later, the issue is still salient, although the self-image is decidedly female (Figure 13-3e).

Barrier Pictures

"Reality and Dayhouse" (Figure 13-4a) was drawn in 1982. Cara, of course, had no idea of its meaning at the time. In retrospect, this picture was thought by Cara to have been drawn to "qualify for insurance through suicidal imagery." Here one sees the juxtaposition of inner feelings (on the right) and the external persona (on the left). Again, elements of the system are foreshadowed in the balloons and split costume of the clown. A similar composition is seen in a much later drawing (Figure 13-4b), which illustrates

FIGURE 13-4a
(1982)

an internal conflict between groups of alter personalities. "Jail" refers to the issue of containment within the system, as well as imprisonment in the hospital.

Cara drew Figures 13-4c and 13-4d in the late 1980s. Both pictures are cross-section images illustrating various types of protective barriers within her system; the latter image depicts more permeable boundaries. According to Cara, "selves are starting to leak through, and there are some selves that are closer to Cara . . . and others that are closer to 'social'." The black wedge shows her connection to the outside world so that she knows what is going on in the outside world when she wants to. In both images, the client makes the distinction between the core Cara and the others who protect her. In the former image, all the barriers are quite thick and dense.

FIGURE 13-4b

(c. 1988)

FIGURE 13-4c
(c. 1988)

FIGURE 13-4d
(1987)

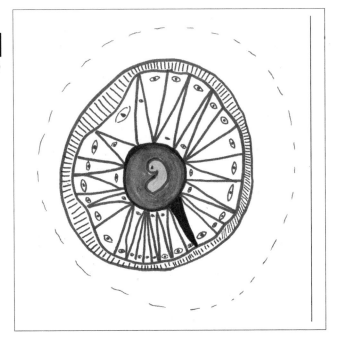

FIGURE 13-4e
(c. 1988)

FIGURE 13-4f
(1989)

"Me real, them not real" (Figure 13-4e) is not about the distinction between the client and her alters, as might be assumed. Instead, this picture, drawn in the late 1980s, shows the barrier that is the result of internal sibling rivalry. Some time later, however, Figure 13-4f was drawn. This x-ray image literally gives us a window into the client's inner world; in it, the brick wall of amnesia is crumbling, allowing for flow of communication between parts of self.

Threat Pictures

One of a series of balloonman pictures, Figure 13-5a, drawn in 1981, was thought to include representations of feelings within each balloon. Now, with the benefit of decoded information, the configurations can be understood to represent families within the client's system. Referring to the vulnerability of the person with MPD, the picture was titled, "Anybody got a pin?" The 1987 version of the drawing (Figure 13-5b) more clearly

FIGURE 13-5a
(1981)

FIGURE 13-5b
(1987)

FIGURE 13-5c
(1981)

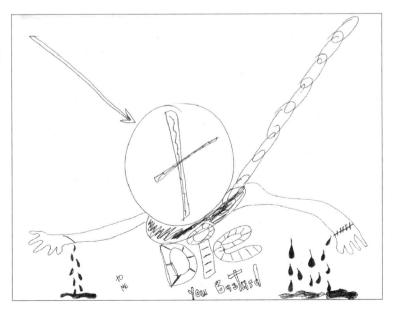

illustrates the ominous title of the 1981 picture. Here, each balloon is divided into four sections, and the group surrounds the central balloon, which is drawn with the core symbol. The threat of the sharpened pin to the balloons is a subtle allusion to the power of certain parts of self to wreak destructive havoc within the system.

Two other images drawn six years apart show the continuity of threat over time. Figure 13-5c, titled "Die you bastard," is inscribed "to me" in tiny letters at the lower left. The familiar generic figure and chain appear, as well as segmentation (in the lettering), which appears throughout Cara's work. The picture was thought to be self-destructive (in the suicidal sense) in 1981, while in 1987, "The Future to the Basturds (sic)" (Figure 13-5d) was understood as a depiction of rivalry within the MPD system.

FIGURE 13-5d
(1987)

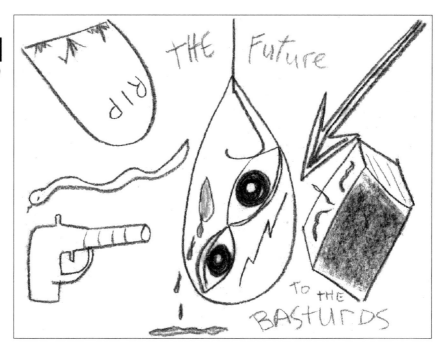

Two other drawings were made about nine years apart; both use pointing arrows to signify threat. Figure 13-5e relies on isolation of a blindfolded protagonist perched atop a diving board to point up the pressure that develops internally from threats. The body designs and sea of shards allude to multiplicity within an individual subject; years later, after her diagnosis was known, the threat was aimed at a plural target (Figure 13-5f). Figure 13-5g is more explicit than these two images. Here, a dagger is placed at the chest of a frightened supine child; "I'm going to kill you and you better not cry" is the internalized warning of an adult perpetrator. The table on which the child lies has a tombstone adjacent to it, almost as if it were a bed's headboard.

FIGURE 13-5e
(1980)

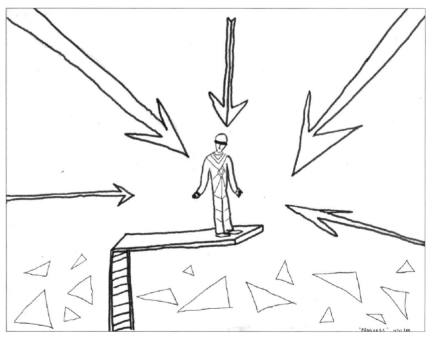

FIGURE 13-5f
(1989)

FIGURE 13-5g
(1989)

FIGURE 13-6a
(1982)

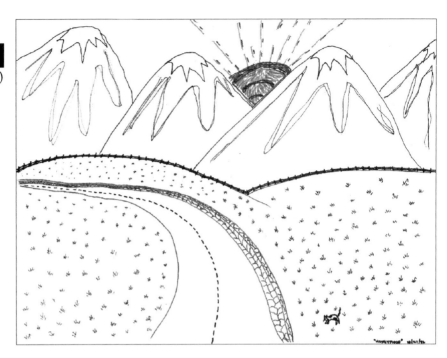

FIGURE 13-6b
(1982)

Induction Pictures

The dotting that characterizes induction pictures is depicted in the context of two landscape drawings. Figure 13-6a takes advantage of a plain stubbled with grass to introduce a randomly patterned field of dots. Figure 13-6b shifts the dotting to a vertical orientation as raindrops isolated around the split, generic figure. The anatomical reference is a somewhat coy conceit of the artist. Both were drawn in 1982.

The next four images illustrate a progression of iconography over a period of years to depict the induction of trance. Figure 13-6c is a colorful crayon drawing that shows the abuser (in the guise of the Big Bad Wolf) coming to snare Cara from her childhood bed. While she fixes visually on the patterned

FIGURE 13-6c

(c. 1985)

floral wallpaper, an imaginary creature comes from under the bed to protect her. Even the fringe around the rug is perseverative and trance inducing. In the next image (Figure 13-6d) an alter personality's persona is rife with dots; her hair, earrings, blouse, and skirt fringe are patterned with polka dots, while her colorful headgear spouts colored dots into the air, as if to externalize her mind state. Figure 13-6e is typical of induction pictures in that it is an abstraction. Emanating from a central point, dots spiral out to fill the page; bright yellow radiating lines complete the composition. The fifth of these six illustrations (Figure 13-6f), unusually colorful for Cara, was painted in the hospital using dental sponges and tempera paints. The springy texture of the sponge-brush facilitated the rhythm of trance induction for her.

FIGURE 13-6d

(1989)

FIGURE 13-6e
(1988)

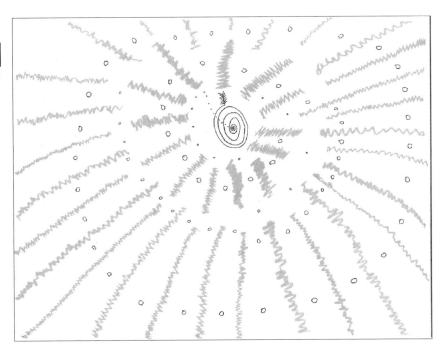

FIGURE 13-6f
(1989)

FIGURE 13-7a
(1980)

FIGURE 13-7b
(1982)

Trance Pictures

Three surreal pictures were drawn over the period of a decade. A grouping of personal symbols appears in each of these pictures as well as in many of the drawings in this chapter. Figure 13-7a, drawn in 1980 (five years before her diagnosis), is essentially an abstraction. It includes the ubiquitous core fetal symbol, chains, an arrow, and spiral. Organized into a Calder-like mobile, now familiar images of the eye, tree, generic figure, and lightning bolt were first drawn in 1982 (Figure 13-7b). Even the fetal symbol was internally layered. The third image (Figure 13-7c), drawn in 1990, contains all of these

FIGURE 13-7c
(1990)

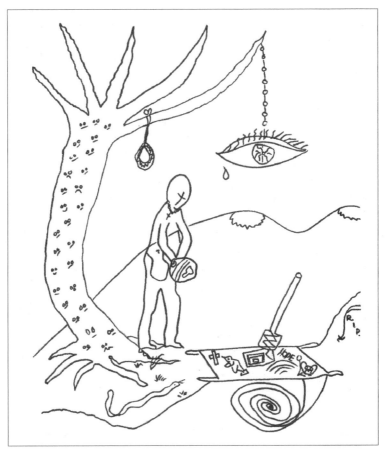

symbols. When this picture was created, Cara was in a state-run facility in which the medical staff did not believe she had MPD. Here one sees the visual exacerbation of her imagery.

Once again, the tree is used as a self-image, although this one is quite traumatized (Figure 13-7d). One extraordinary aspect of this picture, drawn around 1990, is the white silhouette of the client's father, which itself casts a shadow. Many of Cara's symbols appear in the disjointed trance pictures from the late 1980s; Figures 13-7e and 13-7f are typical.

(c. 1990)

FIGURE 13-7e
(1989)

FIGURE 13-7f
(1987)

FIGURE 13-8b
(1982)

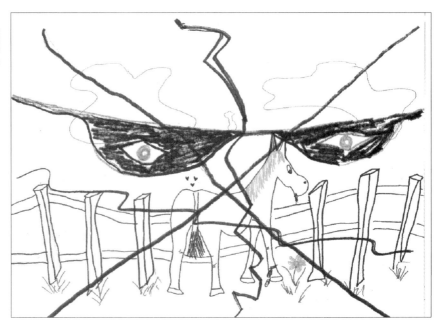

Switching Pictures

Cara says that she drew Figure 13-8a in 1980 in order to "keep her insurance." She states, "A lot of my behavior in the hospital was geared around qualifying for insurance—institutional games you have to play. If I wasn't ready to get out and I couldn't handle life on the outside, then we made a suicide attempt or we made it look like a suicide attempt. A lot of that went on. It was a way of protecting, a way of surviving." In the process of creating bizarre images, she unintentionally disclosed the core symbol (in the kite) and the tree broken at its base. In the artwork of borderline patients, the red "X" would be considered self-destructive, rather than an indicator of the process of switching. Crossing-out was a response to revealing information of which even she was unaware at the time; it nonetheless saved the picture from physical destruction. Figure 13-8b, drawn two years later (but still years before her diagnosis was changed to MPD), reflects a distinctly different drawing approach, which is rather adolescent in quality. Subtle clues to abuse and multiplicity are

FIGURE 13-8c
(1987)

also evidenced in the shackled front hoof and posterior view, the fence barrier, and the tiny figure dangling from the horse's mouth. The overt switch, however, was made during the lunch break following art therapy; the vertical crack in the picture, "X," and menacing mask were drawn over this inadvertent disclosure. Paradoxically, to a knowing viewer, these changes would heighten the original effect.

Two other signs of switching are seen in the next two figures, drawn during Cara's treatment for MPD. Figure 13-8c shows how, even after a significant amount of energy and time have been expended on a drawing, the feelings of another part of self can instigate destruction of that work. Similarly, a disgruntled alter emerged during the creation of Figure 13-8d to contribute an editorial comment.

Figure 13-8e, drawn in 1988, illustrates alters with different levels of graphic development uncomfortably sharing the same page space. Cara

FIGURE 13-8d

(1988)

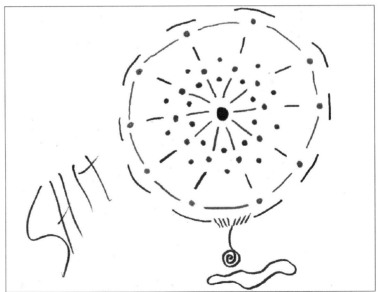

FIGURE 13-8e
(1988)

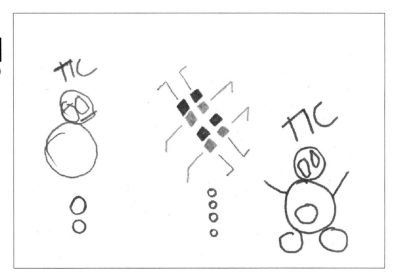

FIGURE 13-8f
(1988)

explained the relative scarcity of switching pictures compared to the other nine categories of this model as "a territorial issue"; different parts do not usually want to share time and space with others, particularly during phases of treatment in which internal cooperation is at a minimum. Collaboration between alter personalities is evidenced in Figures 13-8f and 13-8g. The system configuration inside the balloon (in the former) is clearly drawn by a different part than the rest of the picture. In the latter picture, the decorative patterning on the lower section and at the left was obviously drawn by a different alter than the rest of the picture, as illustrated by the change in drawing styles. Two alters, in fact, signed the reverse side of this picture. Cooperation and collaboration are essential to progress in treatment; in art therapy, older alter personalities will often allow younger ones to color in their drawings for them.

FIGURE 13-8g
(1987)

Abreaction Pictures

The twelve drawings in this section provide a graphic document of one person's journey through traumatic memory. The first surviving image (drawn in the presence of an art therapist) was created in 1980 before client, therapist, or physician considered the diagnosis of MPD; the diagnosis itself was barely in use in the metropolitan Washington area. Further, ritualistic abuse was not discussed (because it was not even considered) at that time. That such a series of pictures comes to the public's attention at this juncture in this field's history is significant, considering the raging arguments among clinicians, academics, and the lay public regarding the nature of memory, traumatic memory recall, and allegations of multi-perpetrator ritualistic abuse (de Mause, 1994; Simon, 1993). Notably, during the early years of treatment, this client received no hypnosis, which is typically targeted as a contaminating factor in these cases (Van Benschoten, 1990). ·

"Suspended Anger" is the title of this enigmatic picture made on June 7, 1980 (Figure 13-9a). Drawn in black and white chalk on red construction

FIGURE 13-9a
(1980)

FIGURE 13-9b
(1981)

FIGURE 13-9c
(1981)

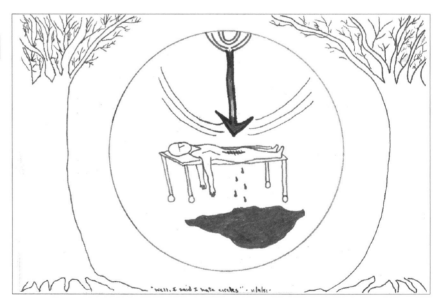

paper, it easily fulfilled the criteria for the art of borderline personality disorder patients. However, the segmented target, generic figures, chains, arrows, and lightning bolts are composed in a way that foreshadows the unfolding of graphic memories. Each picture retains, over a period of eight years, a similar structural and narrative format. The following image (Figure 13-9b), drawn in 1981, is ironically titled "Just Another Day." It adds details of four-point restraints and three overlapping arrows pointing to the stomach.

In response to a mandala assignment, Cara drew a picture that she titled, "Well I Said I Hate Circles" (Figure 13-9a). This image, drawn in 1981, introduced the hanging spear above the body (which is segmented by colors) and the table upon which the body lies. Dead trees guard this perversely sacred space. A child alter drew a more personal perspective in Figure 13-9d some seven years later. Here a blade is suspended by a chain, held by a person's

FIGURE 13-9d
(1988)

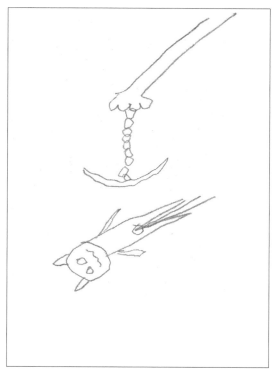

hand. The self-image is reminiscent of a sacrificial animal. Other alters contribute details to the scenario; in Figure 13-9e, through images scratched into fingerpaint, details of the environment emerge from a deep maroon ground. Figure 13-9f depicts a more detached view, with increased details.

A rabbit and abdominal marking appear in Figure 13-9g, and the hanging chain now supports a censer of incense. Collaboration between alters resulted in Figure 13-9h, which attempts to explain the process of events over time: a figure is simultaneously asleep in bed and laying on a table; the latter has a mental image of a broken cross. According to Cara, the tiny creature atop the thought balloon and the alter brandishing the sword at "the gates of hell" (note barrier and flames at left) depict parts of self that emerged to guard and sustain the client through these traumatic events.

FIGURE 13-9e
(c. 1988)

FIGURE 13-9f
(1988)

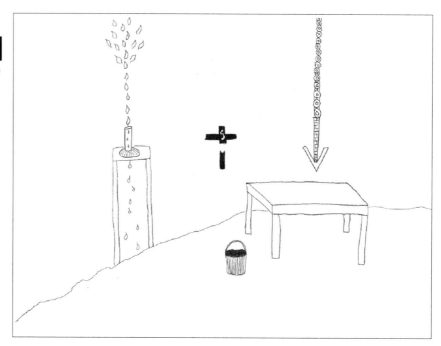

FIGURE 13-9g
(1988)

Seen from an aerial vantage, Figure 13-9i shows a child personality's experience, which includes a guardian angel alter. This drawing introduces the figures of adult perpetrators at the picture's right and left sides. Note the crudely drawn eyeglasses on the figure at the right. Figure 13-9j is another aerial perspective image of the scene, but highly stylized, by an adult personality, done later as part of her ongoing reworking of the trauma.

Still stylized, but almost completely decoded in Figure 13-9k, the nighttime ritual practices of Cara's parents and their accomplices are detailed. These activities included anal penetration with a broken cross, painting the victim with animals' blood, and other sadistic violations. Figure 13-9l represents the scene naturalistically. Note the father's eyeglasses (standing on the right), the dead bird and fish, and other elements that played an important role throughout her art therapy treatment (see Figure 13-7e). The alter who made this uncoded drawing folded it, put it away, and quickly passed it on to the psychiatrist, who stored it. Drawn on June 20, 1988, it was given to the authors shortly thereafter. Across the bottom of the picture is written "They choke me. What does it mean?"

FIGURE 13-9h
(1988)

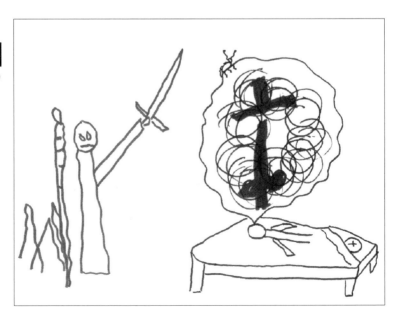

FIGURE 13-9i
(c. 1988)

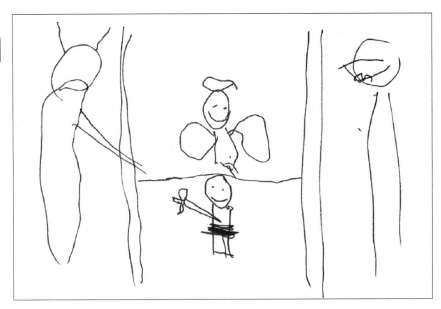

FIGURE 13-9j
(1989)

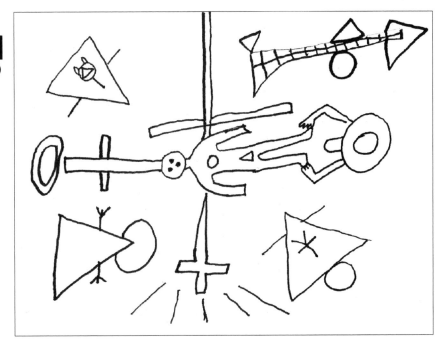

FIGURE 13-9k

(1988)

FIGURE 13-9l

(1988)

THEY CHOKE ME

WHAT DOES IT MEAN

Figure 13-10a is one of the few watercolor paintings ever produced by Cara during treatment. It was done in 1982. Titled "On Being a Woman," this image looks innocent until the vine is identified as the outline of a bird's profile, and the flower as its genital area. Cara pointed out many years after completing this piece that the flower's stem was coding that concealed a penetrating wedge. The butterfly, tiny as it is, suggests the option of fanciful flight from trauma.

"Pop" exclaims the title of the pre-diagnosis chalk pastel drawing in Figure 13-10b. Both the black-haired alter and this media are rare in Cara's work. The girl is making a huge bubble gum bubble, which is about to explode. At another level of meaning, the phallic shape that extends from her mouth reveals that she is, in fact, "blowing pop" (that is, fellating him).

FIGURE 13-10a
(1982)

"Time Bomb" (Figure 13-10c), the alarming title of this 1982 picture, compositionally draws the viewer's attention away from the coded images of fragmentation and multiplicity in the center of the picture. The ticking time bomb was Cara's attempt to communicate the impending explosion in her inner world to her therapist. "You have to understand," she now says, "we couldn't function anymore and we were starting to show. We couldn't hold the pretense of mommy and 4.0 student and executive wife . . . we just broke." Drawn during the mid-eighties, "Freedom of Choice?" (Figure 13-10d) slyly alludes to the client's feelings of helplessness in the face of uncontrollable switching. The "out of order" sign reinforces the brokenness associated with the emotional illness. The various brands of soft drink cans represent the different parts of self.

FIGURE 13-10b

(c. 1984)

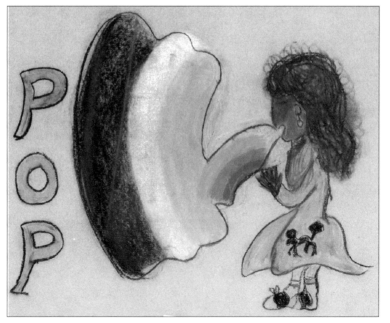

FIGURE 13-10c
(1982)

FIGURE 13-10d
(c. 1985)

FIGURE 13-10e
(1988)

Bubbles are a convenient choice for the coding of dissociation and multiplicity, as many bubbles can come from a single source. Figure 13-10e depicts a young alter climbing steps to nowhere in particular. The floating-away sensation of dissociation is concretized in the ascension of the bubbles.

Figure 13-10f epitomizes the abject terror that survivors of trauma experience at the moment of trauma and across a lifetime. This particular drawing is an anthropomorphization of the tree as self-symbol; its undulating branches are its hair, standing on end in fright. The bulging eyes and gaping mouth scream in horror. Cara draws wounds on each of the many roots of the tree, suggesting her various traumatized alters. The trunk of the tree, which is commonly associated with the physical body, incorporates the eyes and mouth, which could also be seen as breasts and vagina. In this way, she was able to tell about her abuse and multiplicity without talking.

FIGURE 13-10f

(1988)

Conclusion More than one thousand drawings and paintings produced over a decade by this client offered a unique opportunity to study code making and breaking during the course of psychiatric treatment. For many, seeing is believing, and so it is with this special body of artwork.

Significantly, Carol Cox kept notes on Cara's creations and responses at that time. She was not in any way on the lookout for material indicating DID. Cox (1985) concluded that the recurrence of the fetal symbol in her client's art predicted each suicide attempt and related her self-destructive behavior to self-esteem and other issues of the incest survivor. Multiplicity, in fact, was not considered. Except for a handful of contemporary pioneers, few clinicians at that point in time made the conceptual leap from the long-term aftereffects of childhood trauma to this ostensibly rare disorder (Greaves, 1993).

Cara externalized, explored, and synthesized her dissociated traumas and her dissociative response through artmaking. In this way, her productions illustrate many of the benefits of art therapy. As an investigation in personal symbolism, the evolution of her imagery is worthy of further study. The pictorial unfolding of Cara's memories of ritualistic abuse deserve particular attention. This series of pictures challenges the viewer to consider this issue anew. None of the widely published cases such as Sybil (Schreiber, 1973), Billy Milligan (Keyes, 1981), or Eve (Sizemore & Pittillo, 1977) included imagery similar to Cara's in the reproductions of their subject's artwork. Cara's pictures, however, are nonetheless echoed again and again in the creative productions of thousands of other clients diagnosed with DID who claim similar histories and who have never been exposed to her work. Although drawings can never be assumed to be proof of historical fact, this pictorial case study is significant.

Once seen, even if only for a brief moment,
the image is never returned to its
previous state; an aspect of consciousness
is forever changed.

– Joy Schaverien

Afterword

As the process of establishing dissociative identity disorder as a distinct diagnosis with proven validity and reliability continues (Loewenstein, 1993; North, Ryall, Ricci, & Wetzel, 1993; Ross, Courtois, & Elliott, 1994), art therapists have a role to play in differentiating and identifying DID in the psychiatric population through art (Cohen & Cox, 1989; Mills & Cohen, 1993). Here we have made our contribution to this process by organizing the art of people with DID into recognizable categories, based on our empirical observations.

Artwork that fits into the ten categories may appear in any order and frequency during the course of treatment. When a particular type occurs repeatedly in a client's art during a circumscribed time period, the therapist should attend to specific issues related to that category. For instance, some clients produce one abreaction picture after another; for these clients, containment is crucial, and working with barrier imagery may prove helpful.

Since input from both verbal and nonverbal modalities must be taken into account (Cohen, Cox, Mills, & Jacobson, 1994), it is essential that the art therapist and the client's primary psychotherapist maintain an ongoing dialogue. As these therapists exchange observations, they are likely to find parallels between talk therapy and art therapy. For example, artmaking strategies serve as a framework for the organization of information in communication, much like grammar in language; styles in art correspond with aspects of behavior, as do volume and intonation in speech, and gesticulation and body posture in demeanor; and meaning in art is revealed through a synthesis of what is represented in process, structure, and content elements, as well as what is implied, as in written language.

Artmaking strategies and styles that characterize habitual modes of artmaking, or those that appear at critical points in treatment, indicate the tenor of the client's inner world. Expressionism, for instance, may suggest a highly agitated or depressed affective state, while elementalism may reflect either detachment or developmental limitations. Especially when the client's art style is incongruent with her behavior or manifest expression, such clues are helpful. As artmaking strategies and styles can be combined and re-combined like elements in chemical reactions, deciphering the client's communication can be facilitated by closely examining the artwork's *active ingredients*. Naturally, one must use common sense in making judgments about what one sees.

Our integrative method refers specifically to the synthesis or integration of meaning in therapeutic artwork. Influenced deeply by our understanding of dissociative identity disorder, this method, if applied thoughtfully and paced carefully, may facilitate the patient's integration process. Keen observers using the integrative method may find interesting correlations between particular types of alters, dynamics at therapeutic junctures, and the use of certain media, strategies, styles, or categories. For instance, during the diagnostic phase, one client abruptly changed the type of paper and drawing materials she used; this was an early sign of her multiplicity, with metamorphosis of pictorial content following soon after. Switching behaviors may manifest clearly in pictures long before they do so behaviorally. It is important to bear in mind, however, that *no single picture* should ever constitute the *sole basis* for a diagnostic judgment. In fact, as pictures accumulate into the client's body of work, "the individual picture is no longer seen as a single unit but a part of a whole sequence of pictures which belong together" (Schaverien, 1992, p. 49).

Over the last five years feedback from therapists using this multileveled approach has influenced our revision of the model; we look forward to hearing of the experiences of others. Thus far, therapists from every part of the United States and in Holland (Heijtmajer & Cohen, 1993) have reported successfully recognizing the ten categories in their clients' work. More formal research is needed to study the prevalence of these categories in DID as well as other psychiatric populations (see Kress, 1992; Mangini, Havlena, & Berenson, 1991).

Guidelines for the practice of art therapy and the well-informed use of art productions in treatment with this population are well beyond the scope of this book. These issues have been discussed elsewhere (Cohen, Cox, Mills, & Jacobson, 1994; Frye & Gannon, 1993; Kluft, 1993; Simonds, 1994). Professionals are reminded to refrain from working beyond their area of competence, especially when clients present art unbidden. It remains a given that art will be produced during the course of this treatment, if only to relieve the internalized pressure to reveal secrets; at such times the therapist's ability to respond skillfully and appropriately to the client is crucial to the outcome of the therapeutic process.

Antonin Artaud, the controversial surrealist writer, was no stranger to the therapeutic effects of making art; the walls of the room in which he lived were covered with his own drawings. In fact, Artaud found art indispensable to alleviate his own suffering during nine years of psychiatric institutionalization; he wrote, "no one has ever written, painted, sculpted, built, or invented except literally to get out of hell" (cited in MacGregor, 1989, p. 285). According to Artaud, a madman is one who "society did not want to hear and . . . prevented from uttering certain intolerable truths" (p. 284). Our clients find themselves in the position of the madman, shouting in their own way the intolerable truths of physical, sexual, and emotional abuse and exploitation of children in modern society. They demand that viewers bear witness to their personal realities, thereby making themselves vulnerable to social stigmatization.

We have seen the courage and resiliency of the human psyche reflected in the artwork of people with multiple personality disorder. We hope the generosity of those who contributed their therapeutic artwork to this study will benefit those whose lives have followed similar paths as well as those people who have dedicated themselves to their support and treatment.

Glossary

Abreaction: The discharge of energy involved in recalling an event that has been repressed because it was consciously intolerable. The experience is one of reliving the trauma as if it were happening in the present, complete with physical and emotional manifestations. A therapeutic effect sometimes occurs through partial discharge or desensitization of the painful emotions and increased insight (Cohen, Giller, & W., 1991). Abreaction can happen spontaneously (see also **flashbacks**) or can be therapeutically induced through verbal suggestion or hypnosis.

Affect: The psychiatric term for any experience of feeling or emotion (Goldenson, 1984).

Alter: (Also known as a "personality" in the field of dissociative disorders) An entity with a firm, persistent, and well-founded sense of self, and a characteristic and consistent pattern of behavior and feelings in response to given stimuli. It must have a range of functions, a range of emotional responses, and a significant life history (of its own existence) (Cohen, Giller, & W., 1991).

Amnestic barrier: Obstacles to remembering that may be caused by compartmentalization of traumatic material that is too painful or overwhelming.

Anthropomorphism: The attribution of human characteristics to nonhuman entities (Goldenson, 1984).

Artmaking strategies: Basic approaches to picture-making in which essential elements are structurally manipulated to convey meaning. There are seven categories, each comprised of two approaches (see pp. 6–7).

Coding: An inherent benefit of symbolic expression through art that allows the artist to reveal information while simultaneously concealing it through camouflage or substitution of images. Due largely to the quality of multileveledness, repressed or dissociated material can thus be released to consciousness and expressed through art.

Cognitive distortions: In DID, ways of thinking that are often rigid and stem from the victimized child's attempts to make sense about her unpredictable, overwhelming, and unsafe world. Most common are the notions that each alter is a separate person and that child parts of self are actually children (see also **trance logic**).

Content level: The overt or symbolic subject matter of a picture.

Dissociation: A complex process of change in a person's consciousness that causes a disturbance or alteration in the normally integrative functions of identity, memory, thought, feeling, and experience. Dissociative processes exist on a continuum. At one end are mild dissociative experiences common to most people, such as daydreaming or highway hypnosis; at the other extreme are severe, chronic dissociation states, such as in MPD/DID.

Dissociative identity disorder: The presence of two or more distinct identities or personality states (each with its own relatively enduring pattern of perceiving, relating to, and thinking about the environment and self). At least two of these identities or personality states recurrently take control of the person's behavior, with inability to recall important personal information that is too extensive to be explained by ordinary forgetfulness (DSM-IV).

Flashbacks: A type of spontaneous abreaction common to victims of acute trauma. Also known as "intrusive recall," flashbacks have been categorized into four types: (1) dreams or nightmares; (2) dreams from which the dreamer awakens but remains under the influence of the dream content so that she has difficulty making contact with reality; (3) conscious flashbacks, in which the person may or may not lose contact with reality and which may be accompanied by multisensory hallucinations; and (4) unconscious flashbacks, in which the person "relives" a traumatic event with no awareness at the time or later of the connection between the flashback and the past trauma (Cohen, Giller, & W., 1991).

Gestalt: In art, a form or configuration.

Integrative method: A process for understanding art in which the viewer synthesizes process, structure, and content levels of a picture. With DID art, this includes the ten category model as well.

Isomorphism: Correspondence between an internal (psychic) state and its external manifestation (in art).

Multileveledness: Simultaneous communication of several related and/or contrasting meanings.

Multiple personality disorder: (see **dissociative identity disorder**)

Negative space: The area between lines or shapes in pictorial composition.

Perseveration: The pathological repetition of the same act, idea, work, or phrases (or graphic equivalent in the making of art, e.g., lines or shapes); also an inability to interrupt a task or shift from one task or procedure to another (Goldenson, 1984).

Primary process: In psychoanalytic theory, a type of unconscious mental activity characteristic of childhood thinking and dreams, in which impulses are enacted instinctively in an uninhibited fashion, resulting in imagery not governed by constrictions of consensual reality or logic.

Process level: The client's behavior and verbalizations while making artwork, as well as the dialogue between observer-therapist and artist-client about the artwork after it is completed.

Schema: In art, a configuration used habitually for representing a concept.

Structure level: The most basic building blocks, artmaking strategies, and styles of a picture.

Style: A distinctive mode of expression determined by the choice of artmaking strategies. Four styles are discussed in this book: *naturalism, elementalism, expressionism,* and *surrealism* (see p. 7).

Switching: The process of changing from one alter personality to another. Switching may be stimulated by an internal perception or by an external, environmental **trigger**. Individuals with DID have varying degrees of control over the process, gaining more control as treatment progresses. Switches may be accompanied by physiological changes (e.g., in posture, facial expressions, and voice or speech patterns) and by psychological changes (e.g., in mood, behavioral age, and level of intelligence) (Cohen, Giller, & W., 1991).

System: Here, the structure of relationships within the internal world of an individual who has DID. Although each person's system is unique, there are several recurring metaphors used by clients to describe how they function. Examples include stages, spotlights, tunnels, houses, and levels. It is often helpful for a person with DID to make a map or diagram of his/her internal personality system.

Ten category model: Groupings into which art by people with DID commonly falls. It can be used to identify those with the disorder and provide a framework for the exploration and explication of their art and life (see p. 17).

Trance logic: A way of thinking, associated with the hypnotic state, in which irrational and illogical beliefs are uncritically maintained and literal mindedness prevails. Multileveledness in art fosters the externalization of trance logic (see also **cognitive distortions**).

Trauma: Any sudden injury or damage to an organism. Psychological trauma is an event that is outside the range of usual human experience and is so seriously distressing as to overwhelm the mind's defenses and cause lasting emotional harm. Most individuals with MPD have been victims of repeated child abuse, rape, and/or torture, but other kinds of psychological trauma, including severe neglect, can also cause MPD.

Trigger: An event, object, person, etc., that sets in motion a series of thoughts or reminds a person of some aspect of his/her traumatic past. The person may be unaware of what is "triggering" the memory (e.g., loud noises, a particular color, piece of music, odor). Connected with brainwashing, a trigger may elicit a specific command message.

Bibliography

Aldridge-Morris, R. (1989). *Multiple personality: An exercise in deception.* Hillsdale, NJ: Erlbaum.

American Psychiatric Association. (1994). Diagnostic and statistical manual of mental disorders (4th ed.). Washington, DC: Author.

Arnheim, R. (1974). *Art and visual perception: A psychology of the creative eye* (2nd ed.). Berkeley: University of California Press.

Beahrs, J. O. (1982). *Unity and multiplicity: Multiple consciousness of self in hypnosis, psychiatric disorder and mental health.* New York: Brunner/Mazel.

Bender, L. (1952). *Child psychiatric techniques: Diagnostic and therapeutic approaches to normal and abnormal development through patterned, expressive, and group behavior.* Springfield, IL: Charles C Thomas.

Bernstein, E. M., & Putnam, F. W. (1986). Development, reliability, and validity of a dissociation scale. *Journal of Nervous and Mental Disease, 174,* 727-735.

Birren, F. (1978). *Color psychology and color therapy.* Secaucus, NJ: Citadel.

Boon, S., & Draijer, N. (1993). *Multiple personality disorder in the Netherlands: A study on reliability and validity of the diagnosis.* Amsterdam: Swets & Zeitlinger.

Braude, S. (1992). *First person plural: Multiple personality and the philosophy of mind.* London: Routledge.

Braun, B. G. (1983). Psychophysiologic phenomena in multiple personality disorder. *American Journal of Clinical Hypnosis, 26,* 124-137.

Braun, B. G. (1988). The BASK model of dissociation. *Dissociation, 1*(1), 4-23.

Carlson, E. B., & Putnam, F. W. (1993). An update on the dissociative experiences scale. *Dissociation,* 6(1), 16-27.

Carroll, L. (1866). *Alice's adventures in wonderland.* London: Macmillan.

Carroll, L. (1872). *Through the looking glass.* London: Macmillan.

Chu, J. A. (1991). The repetition compulsion revisited: Reliving dissociated trauma. *Psychotherapy, 28,* 327-332.

Cirlot, J. E. (1962). *A dictionary of symbols.* New York: Philosophical Library.

Cohen, B. M. (Speaker). (1993). *Art and MPD: Uncommon realities* (Cassette Recording No. 834-93-13). Alexandria, VA: Audio Transcripts, Ltd.

Cohen, B. M. (in press). Art and the dissociative paracosm: Uncommon realities. In L. Michaelson & W. Ray (Eds.), *Handbook of dissociation: Theoretical, empirical and clinical perspectives*. New York: Plenum.

Cohen, B. M., & Cox, C. T. (1989). Breaking the code: Identification of multiplicity through art productions. *Dissociation, 2*(3), 132-137.

Cohen, B. M., Cox, C. T., & Mills, A., & Jacobson, M. (Speakers). (1994). Aspects of artmaking and MPD (Cassette Recording No. 51-941-94A). Alexandria, VA: Audio Transcripts, Ltd.

Cohen, B. M., Cox, C. T., Mills, A., & Sobol, B. (Speakers). (1990). Art by abuse survivors: A lifecycle (Cassette Recording No. 569-05-90). Alexandria, VA: Audio Transcripts, Ltd.

Cohen, B. M., Giller, E., & W., L. (Eds.). (1991). *Multiple personality disorder from the inside out*. Baltimore: Sidran Press.

Cohen, B. M., Hammer, J. S., & Singer, S. (1988). The Diagnostic Drawing Series: A systematic approach to art therapy evaluation and research. *The Arts in Psychotherapy, l5*(1), 11-21.

Coons, P. (1984). The differential diagnosis of multiple personality disorder: A comprehensive review. *Psychiatric Clinics of North America, 7*, 51-65.

Coons, P. (Speaker). (1988). The use of patient productions in the diagnosis and treatment of patients with multiple personality/dissociative states (Cassette Recording No. X1a-436-88). Alexandria, VA: Audio Transcripts, Ltd.

Courtois, C. A. (1988). *Healing the incest wound: Adult survivors in therapy*. New York: Norton.

Cox, C. T. (1985). *Themes of self-destruction: Indicators of suicidal ideation in art therapy*. Paper presented at the American Art Therapy Association Sixteenth Annual Conference, New Orleans, LA.

Cox, C. T., & Fleming, M. (1986). *Somatic distress: Report on results from the 1983 conference workshops*. Paper presented at the American Art Therapy Association Seventeenth Annual Conference, Los Angeles, CA.

Cox, M. (1992). *Children's drawings*. New York: Penguin Books.

Crabtree, A. (1992). Dissociation and memory: A two-hundred-year perspective. *Dissociation, 5*(3), 150-154.

Dax, E. C. (1953). *Experimental studies in psychiatric art*. London: Faber and Faber.

Dell, P. F. (1988). Professional skepticism about multiple personality. *Journal of Nervous and Mental Disease, 176*, 528-531.

de Mause, L. (Ed.). (1994). Special issue: Cult abuse of children: Witch hunt or reality? *Journal of Psychohistory, 21*(4), 373-518.

Dondis, D. A. (1973). *A primer of visual literacy*. Cambridge, MA: MIT Press.

Franklin, J. (1990). Dreamlike thought and dream mode processes in the formation of personalities in MPD. *Dissociation, 3*(2), 70-80.

Freud, S. (1958). Formulations regarding the two principles in mental functioning. In J. Strachey (Ed. and Trans.), *The standard edition of the complete psychological works of Sigmund Freud* (Vol. 12, pp. 215-226). New York: Norton. (Original work published 1911)

Frye, B., & Gannon, L. (1993). The use, misuse, and abuse of art with dissociative/multiple personality disorder patients. *Dissociation*, 6(2/3), 188-192.

Fuhrman, N. L. (1988). Art, interpretation, and multiple personality disorder. *Dissociation*, 1(4), 33-40.

Fuhrman, N. L. (1993). Art and multiple personality disorder: A developmental approach to treatment. In E.S. Kluft (Ed.), *Expressive and functional therapies in the treatment of multiple personality disorder* (pp. 23-38). Springfield: Charles C Thomas.

Gelinas, D. J. (1983). The persisting negative effects of incest. *Psychiatry*, 46, 313-332.

Giedion, S. (1962). *The eternal present: The beginnings of art*. New York: Pantheon Books.

Glass, J. M. (1993). *Shattered selves: Multiple personality in a postmodern world*. Ithaca, NY: Cornell University Press.

Goettman, C., Greaves, G. B., & Coons, P.M. (Eds.). (1994). *Multiple personality and dissociation, 1791-1992: A complete bibliography* (2nd ed.). Lutherville, MD: Sidran Press.

Goldenson, R. M. (Ed.). (1984). *Longman dictionary of psychology and psychiatry*. New York: Longman.

Golomb, C. (1992). *The child's creation of a pictorial world*. Berkeley, CA: University of California Press.

Greaves, G. B. (1993). A history of multiple personality disorder. In R. P. Kluft and C. G. Fine (Eds.), *Clinical perspectives on multiple personality disorder*, (pp. 355-380). Washington, DC: American Psychiatric Press.

Heijtmajer, O. A., & Cohen, B. M. (Speakers). (1993). MPD and the Diagnostic Drawing Series: A Dutch replication study (Cassette Recording No. 860-93-4A). Alexandria, VA: Audio Transcripts, Ltd.

Herman, J. L. (1992). *Trauma and recovery*. New York: Basic Books.

Hilgard, E. R. (1977). *Divided consciousness: Multiple controls in human thought and action*. New York: Wiley.

Hillman, J. (1977). *Re-visioning psychology*. New York: Harper & Row.

Horowitz, M. J. (1970). *Image formation and cognition*. New York: Appleton-Century Crofts.

Jung, C. G. (1964). *Man and his symbols*. Garden City, NY: Doubleday.

Kagin, S. (1969) *The effects of structure on the painting of retarded youth*. Unpublished master's thesis, University of Tulsa, Tulsa, OK.

Kagin, S., & Lusebrink, V. B. (1978). The expressive therapies continuum. *Art Psychotherapy*, 5(4), 171-179.

Kellogg, J. (1984). *Mandala: Path of beauty*. Lightfoot, VA: MARI.

Kemp, K., Gilbertson, A.D., & Torem, M. (1988). The differential diagnosis of multiple personality disorder from borderline personality disorder. *Dissociation*, 1(4), 41-46.

Keyes, D. (1981). *The minds of Billy Milligan*. New York: Random House.

Kluft, E. S. (Ed.). (1993). *Expressive and functional therapies in the treatment of multiple personality disorder*. Springfield, IL: Charles C Thomas.

Kluft, R. P. (1985). Natural history of multiple personality disorder. In R.P. Kluft (Ed.), *Childhood antecedents of multiple personality disorder* (pp. 197-238). Washington, DC: American Psychiatric Press, Inc.

Kluft, R.P. (1990). Dissociation and subsequent vulnerability: A preliminary study. *Dissociation, 3*(3), 167-173

Kluft, R. P., & Fine, C. (Eds.). (1993). *Clinical perspectives on multiple personality disorder*. Washington, DC: American Psychiatric Press, Inc.

Kramer, E. (1979). *Childhood and art therapy: Notes on theory and application*. New York: Schocken Books.

Kreitler, H., & Kreitler, S. (1972). *Psychology of the arts*. Durham, NC: Duke University Press.

Kress, T. (Speaker). (1992). The Diagnostic Drawing Series and multiple personality disorder: A validation study (Cassette Recording No. 55). Denver, CO: National Audio Video.

Kwiatkowska, H.Y. (1978). *Family therapy and evaluation through art*. Springfield, IL: Charles C Thomas.

Langer, S. (1953). *Feeling and form*. New York: Scribner's.

Lifton, R. J. (1993). *The protean self: Human resilience in an age of fragmentation*. New York: Basic Books.

Loewenstein, R. J. (Ed.). (1991). Multiple personality disorder. *Psychiatric Clinics of North America, 14*, 489-791.

Loewenstein, R. J. (Speaker). (1993). Current research on multiple personality disorders: The validity of MPD (Cassette Recording No. XIII-860-93). Alexandria, VA: Audio Transcripts, Ltd.

Lowenfeld, V., & Brittain, W. L. (1987). *Creative and mental growth* (8th ed.). New York: Macmillan.

Lüscher, M. (1969). *The Lüscher Color Test*. New York: Random House.

Lusebrink, V. B. (1990). *Imagery and visual expression in psychotherapy*. New York: Plenum.

MacGregor, J. M. (1989). *The discovery of the art of the insane*. Princeton, NJ: Princeton University Press.

Mangini, L., Havlena, J., & Berenson, C. (Speakers). (1991). Prevalence of childhood dissociative disorder in a clinic population (Cassette Recording No. 683-91-VIIId). Alexandria, VA: Audio Transcripts, Ltd.

Mersky, H. (1992). The manufacture of personalities: The production of multiple personality disorder. *British Journal of Psychiatry, 160*, 327-340.

Miller, D. (1994). *Women who hurt themselves: A book of hope and understanding*. New York: Basic Books.

Mills, A., & Cohen, B. M. (1993). Facilitating the identification of multiple personality disorder through art: The Diagnostic Drawing Series. In E.S. Kluft (Ed.), *Expressive and functional therapies in the treatment of multiple personality disorder* (pp. 39-66). Springfield: Charles C Thomas.

Mills, A., Cohen, B. M., & Kijak, A. (1994). An introduction to the Diagnostic Drawing Series: A standardized tool for diagnostic and clinical use. *Art Therapy, 11*(2), 105-110.

Murray, P., & Murray, L. (1959). *A dictionary of art and artists.* Baltimore: Penguin Books.

Nathanson, D. (1992). *Shame and pride: Affect, sex, and the birth of the self.* New York: Norton.

North, C. S., Ryall, J. M., Ricci, D. A., & Wetzel, R. D. (1993). *Multiple personalities, multiple disorders: Psychiatric classification and media influence.* New York: Oxford University Press.

Orne, M. T. (1959). The nature of hypnosis: Artifact and essence. *Journal of Abnormal and Social Psychology, 58,* 277-299.

Putnam, F. W. (1989). *Diagnosis and treatment of multiple personality disorder.* New York: Guilford.

Putnam, F. W. (1991). Dissociative disorders in children and adolescents: A developmental perspective. *The Psychiatric Clinics of North America, 14*(3), 519-531.

Putnam, F. W., Guroff, J. J., Silberman, E. K., Barban, L. & Post, R. M. (1986). The clinical phenomenology of multiple personality: A review of 100 recent cases. *Journal of Clinical Psychiatry, 47,* 285-293.

Rankin, A. (1994). Tree drawings and trauma indicators: A comparison of past research with current findings from the Diagnostic Drawing Series. *Art Therapy, 11*(2), 127-130.

Reid, L. A. (1969). *Meaning in the arts.* London: Allen Lane.

Rhyne, J. (1979). *Drawings as personal constructs.* Unpublished doctoral thesis, University of California at Santa Cruz.

Rivera, M. A. (1991). Multiple personality disorder and the social system: 185 cases. *Dissociation, 4*(2), 79-82.

Robbins, A., & Sibley, L. B. (1976). *Creative art therapy.* New York: Brunner/Mazel.

Ross, C. A. (1989). *Multiple personality disorder: Diagnosis, clinical features, and treatment.* New York: Wiley.

Ross, C. A., Heber, S., Norton, G. R., Anderson, D., Anderson, G., & Barchet, P. (1989). The dissociative disorders interview schedule: A structured interview. *Dissociation, 2*(3), 169-189.

Ross, C. A., Courtois, C. A., & Elliott, D. M. (Speakers). (1994). Current abuse research: Strengths and limitations (Cassette Recording No. 05-941-94A). Alexandria, VA: Audio Transcripts, Ltd.

Rubin, J. (1978). *Child art therapy.* New York: Van Nostrand Reinhold.

Rubin, J. (1984). *The art of art therapy.* New York: Brunner/Mazel.

Rubin, J. (1987). *Approaches to art therapy: Theory and technique.* New York: Brunner/Mazel.

Schachtel, E. G. (1943). On color and affect: Contributions to an understanding of Rorschach's test. *Psychiatry, 6,* 393-409.

Schaverien, J. (1992). *The revealing image: Analytical art psychotherapy in theory and practice.* London: Tavistock/Routledge.

Schreiber, F. R. (1973). *Sybil*. Chicago, IL: Henry Regnery Company.

Seiden, D. (Speaker). (1994). Art and the brain (Cassette Recording No. 67-149). Denver, CO: National Audio Video.

Simon, R. (Ed.). (1993). The false memory debate. *Family Therapy Networker*, September-October issue.

Simonds, S. L. (1994). *Bridging the silence: Nonverbal modalities in the treatment of adult survivors of childhood sexual abuse*. New York: Norton.

Sizemore, C. C., & Pittillo, E. S. (1977). *I'm Eve*. Garden City, NY: Doubleday.

Sobol, B., & Cox, C. T. (1991). *Art and childhood dissociation: Research with sexually abused children*. Paper presented at the American Psychiatric Association's 43rd Institute on Hospital and Community Psychiatry, Los Angeles, CA.

Sobol, B., & Cox, C. T. (Speakers). (1992). Art and childhood dissociation: Research with sexually abused children (Cassette Recording No. 59-144). Denver, CO: National Audio Video.

Spiegel, D. (1990). Trauma, dissociation, and hypnosis. In R.P. Kluft (Ed.), *Incest-related syndromes of adult psychopathology* (pp. 247-261). Washington, DC: American Psychiatric Press, Inc.

Spiegel, D. (Speaker). (1991). Dissociation during trauma: Borrowing from the future to pay for the past (Cassette Recording No. 1A-683-91). Alexandria, VA: Audio Transcripts, Ltd.

Spiegel, H., & Spiegel, D. (1978). *Trance and treatment*. New York: Basic Books.

Spring, D. (1993). Artistic symbolic language and the treatment of multiple personality disorder. In E.S. Kluft (Ed.), *Expressive and functional therapies in the treatment of multiple personality disorder* (pp. 85-100). Springfield: Charles C Thomas.

Steinberg, M., Rounsaville, B., & Cicchetti, D. V. (1990). The structured clinical interview for DSM-III-R dissociative disorders: Preliminary report on a new diagnostic instrument. *American Journal of Psychiatry, 147* (1), 76-82.

Torem, M., Gilbertson, A. D., & Light, V. (1990). Indications of physical, sexual, and verbal victimization in projective tree drawings. *Journal of Clinical Psychology, 46*(6), 900-906.

Ulman, E., & Levy, B. (1975). An experimental approach to the judgment of psychopathology from paintings. In E. Ulman & P. Dachinger (Eds.), *Art therapy in theory and practice* (pp. 393-402). New York: Schocken Books.

Van Benschoten, S.C. (1990). Multiple personality disorder and satanic ritual abuse: The issue of credibility. *Dissociation, 3*(1), 22-30.

van der Kolk, B.A. (Ed.). (1987). *Psychological trauma*. Washington, DC: American Psychiatric Press, Inc.

Van Sommers, P. (1984). *Drawing and cognition*. London: Cambridge University Press.

Wadeson, H. (1980). *Art psychotherapy*. New York: Wiley.

Watkins, H.H., & Watkins, J.G. (1993). Ego state therapy in the treatment of dissociative disorders. In R.P. Kluft & C.G. Fine (Eds.), *Clinical perspectives on multiple personality disorder* (pp. 277-299). Washington, DC: American Psychiatric Press, Inc.

Wilson, L. (1987). Symbolism and art therapy: Theory and clinical practice. In J. Rubin (Ed.), *Approaches to art therapy: Theory and technique* (pp. 44-62). New York: Brunner/Mazel.

Index

Cross-reference of Artists and Their Artwork

tree images in, 78
Franklin, J., 145, 146
Freud, S., 145
Frye, B., xiv, 293
Fuhrman, N. L., 171, 195
funnel images, 137

Gannon, L., xiv, 293
Gelinas, D. J., 221
gender conflict, 71
gender representation, 255
genital/sexual images, 35, 71
  in abreaction pictures, 183, 189
  in alert pictures, 226, 227, 231, 233, 285
  self-harm images in switching picture, 205
Giedion, S., 127
Gilbertson, A. D., 35, 253
Giller, E., xiv, 295, 298
Glass, J. M., 62
Goettman, C., xv
Goldenson, R. M., 295, 296, 297
Golomb, C., 218
Greaves, G. B., xv, 289
green, 9, 45, 63, 87, 99, 129, 132, 151, 157, 201, 215, 237
grey, 28, 40, 65, 68, 138, 225
groups of figures
  in barrier picture, 89
  in fragmentation picture, 77
  in system pictures, 22, 26
Guroff, J., xv, 86

hallucination, 79
Hammer, J. S., xviii
hand images, 97, 103, 111, 157, 199
  in abreaction picture, 181
  in threat picture, 123
Havlena, J., 293
headaches, 43
Heber, S., xv
Heijtmajer, O. A., 292
helplessness, 173
Herman, J. L., 221, 222
hidden words, 96
hiding, images of, 173
Hilgard, E. R., 81
Hillman, J., 8
Horowitz, M. J., 166
house images, 87, 163, 211
hyperarousal. see flooding
hypnosis, 145

images within images, 237
induction pictures, 129-41
  abstract images in, 266
  case study, 265-66
  characteristics, 17

clinical significance, 127-28, 142, 143
color in, 142
content, 127-28
to control state shifts, 132-36, 139, 141, 142-43
elementalism in, 142, 143
structure and meaning, 129-41
style, 143
symbols in, 142
trance pictures vs., 147, 166
injury, images of, 209
integrative method
  clinical role, 13
  conceptual basis, 2-3, 297
  determining meaning in, 10-13
  therapeutic goals, 2
interpretation of art
  art as irreducible, 10
  clinician role, 1-2, 5
  color as content, 9-10
  content analysis, 8-10, 11
  determining meaning, 10-13
  in DID, xviii-xix
  in integrative method, 2
  process level factors, 5, 11, 13
  structure level analysis, 6-8, 11
  in synthesis of structure and content, 13
  visual literacy in, 2-3
isolation, 172, 235
isomorphism, 2, 3, 297
  retrieval of traumatic material and, 194

Jacobson, M., 291, 293
jail images, 256
Jung, C. G., 8
juxtaposition, 7
  in abreaction picture, 173
  in alert picture, 233
  in barrier pictures, 87, 96, 97, 103, 104, 166
  in chaos pictures, 47, 49
  of color, 9, 10, 68
  in fragmentation pictures, 63, 68, 77
  in induction picture, 141
  in switching pictures, 199, 207, 211, 213, 218
  in system pictures, 23, 28, 41
  in threat pictures, 110, 111, 117, 123, 124, 125
  in trance pictures, 147, 149, 155, 157, 159, 161, 163, 165, 166

Kagin, S., 2, 4
Kellogg, J., 9, 10, 127, 137, 142
Kemp, K., 253
Keyes, D., 195, 289
Kijak, A., xviii, 151
Kluft, E. S., 293
Kluft, R. P., xv, 194, 221
knife images, 35, 67, 213, 215
  in threat pictures, 111, 123, 124

out-of-body perspective, 149, 163, 165, 209, 226

pain images, 10, 50, 52, 53, 69, 95, 97, 115, 153, 179, 199, 238
  in abreaction pictures, 171, 177, 179, 181, 189
paranoid disorders, 33, 40, 49, 109, 115, 149
part-self/part of self, xi
peach-color, 65
perseveration
  in chaos picture, 49
  counting/number images, 40
  in induction pictures, 129, 131, 132, 134, 139, 142-43, 265
  in trance pictures, 147, 151, 152
pharmacotherapy, to resolve chaos state, 44
pink, 68, 85, 87, 135, 147, 152, 157, 179, 181, 183, 189, 215, 233, 237
Pittillo, E. S., 289
polychrome pictures, 7, 59, 183
Post, R. M., xv, 86
post-traumatic stress, 169-70
posture, 172
process level analysis, 5, 11, 13, 297
psychotic art, 49, 52, 71, 87, 123, 209, 211
  DID art vs., 215, 217
  switching pictures vs., 211, 215
  trance pictures vs., 153, 161, 165
purple, 45, 65, 85, 103, 135, 137, 147, 173, 179, 187
Putnam, F. W., xv, 16, 21, 22, 43, 44, 62, 107, 193, 194, 221, 222
puzzle images, 62

rage, 51, 125, 190
randomness, 6, 37, 135, 166, 218
  in chaos pictures, 49, 59
  in fragmentation pictures, 71, 75, 79
  in induction pictures, 127, 132, 142-43, 166
  in switching pictures, 207, 218
  in trance pictures, 147, 152, 161, 166
Rankin, A., 35
recovered memory, 189, 277
red, 15, 39, 45, 49, 50, 51, 52, 53, 65, 67, 68, 69, 77, 93, 95, 97, 99, 109, 111, 113, 115, 117, 124, 149, 153, 157, 159, 171, 175, 177, 179, 181, 183, 187, 189, 201, 215, 233, 238
  black and, 10, 39, 40, 45, 52, 69, 83, 84, 85, 99, 110, 115, 121, 125, 151, 153, 175, 177, 190, 199, 205, 213, 225, 253
  possible meanings, 9
regression, artmaking media in facilitation of, 4
Reid, L. A., 10
repetition of images, 22
repressed material
  in barrier pictures, 91, 96
  cueing, 194
  in DID, 221-22

disposal of artwork and, 218, 219
emergence in abreaction, 185, 187, 189, 190, 191, 279
expression in art, xiv
release of psychic energy in emergence of, 170
  in trance pictures, 167
reveal-conceal conflict, 107-8, 222, 225, 239
Rhyne, J., xxii, 2, 8
Ricci, D. A., 291
ritual abuse, 277
Rivera, M. A., xv
Robbins, A., 5
Ross, C. A., xv, 21, 22, 43, 107, 205, 221, 291
Rounsaville, B., xv
Rubin, J., viii, 5, 218
Ryall, J. M., 291

sadness, 177
Schachtel, E. G., 9
Schaverien, J., 5, 10, 218, 292
schizophrenic art, 75
  abreaction picture vs., 179
  eye images in, 33
  induction pictures vs., 129
  trance pictures vs., 147, 157, 167
Schreiber, F. R., 289
scribbled-over drawings, 201, 218, 219, 273-74
scribbles
  in chaos pictures, 44, 47, 57
  in induction pictures, 127
  in switching pictures, 197
secrecy
  as absence of mouth images, 199, 233
  art therapy and, xvii-xviii, 222
  in DID, xvii-xviii, 221-22
  hiding behavior, 173
  images in barrier pictures, 83, 84
  reveal-conceal conflict, 107-8, 222, 225, 239
  self-harm and, 107-8
  in threat picture content, 109, 113
Seiden, D., 4
self-harm
  clinical significance, 107-8
  etiology, 107
  images in switching pictures, 205
  potential for, 107
  psychic symptoms, 107
  sexual trauma and, 35
  in system rivalry, 261
self image
  as freakish, 248
  gender representation, 255
  in MPD, 23, 155, 193
sequentiality, 6, 27, 31, 40, 41, 89, 131, 133
sexual images. see genital/sexual images
shame, 205

Sibley, L. B., 5
Silberman, E. K., xv, 86
silver, 115, 225
Simon, R., 277
Simonds, S. L., 172, 293
simplicity, 6, 40, 173, 191
Singer, S., xviii
Sizemore, C. C., 289
snake images, 123, 165
Sobol, B., xiv, 127, 147
somatic sensation, 43, 79
  in abreaction pictures, 171, 187, 189
  flooding, 170
  neurological impairment, 131, 211
Spiegel, D., 57, 61, 146, 166
Spiegel, H., 57, 146
spirals, 44, 45, 211, 253
  as images of suicidality, 124, 253
  in induction pictures, 128, 136, 137, 138
Spring, D., 33, 149
star images, 142, 215
Steinberg, M., xv
structure level analysis, 6-8, 11, 297
style
  in abreaction pictures, 19, 171, 190
  in alert pictures, 19, 239
  in barrier pictures, 19, 104
  in chaos pictures, 19, 59
  clinical significance, 292
  defined, 297
  in fragmentation pictures, 19, 79
  in induction pictures, 19, 143
  structure analysis, 7, 11
  in switching pictures, 19, 195, 199, 203, 213,
    217, 218
  in system pictures, 19, 22
  in threat pictures, 19, 125
  in trance pictures, 19, 159, 167
suicidal behavior/ideation
  insurance coverage and, 273
  spiral images and, 124, 253
  in threat pictures, 107, 113, 117
suppression, amnesia vs., 81
surrealism, 19, 33
  in abreaction pictures, 190
  in alert pictures, 226, 236, 238
  in barrier pictures, 87, 96
  characteristics of, 7
  in switching pictures, 209, 211, 213, 217
  in system pictures, 23, 29, 31, 33, 35
  in threat pictures, 117, 121, 123, 125
  in trance pictures, 149, 152, 155, 157, 159,
    161, 165, 166, 269
switching phenomenon
  chaos and, 44
  control strategies, 194-95
  dangers in, 194

defined, 297-98
model of, 193-94
physical symptoms, 43
switching pictures, 197-217
  abstract images in, 207
  alert pictures vs., 239
  analysis of, 218-19
  attempted disposal of, 218, 219
  attempts to conceal alters in, 199
  case study, 273-76
  characteristics, 17, 218
  circumstances of production, 219
  client state in production of, 195, 218
  collaboration among alters in, 276
  conflict among alters in, 218, 219, 276
  diagnostic and therapeutic significance, 195,
    219
  dialogue among alters in, 197
  genital self-mutilation in, 205
  graphic inconsistencies within, 197, 199, 207,
    211, 213, 217, 218
  juxtaposition of images in, 218
  meaning in, 219
  out-of-body experiences in, 209
  scribbled-over images, 197, 201, 218, 219,
    273-74
  serial switching in, 217
  style, 19, 195, 199, 203, 205, 213, 215, 217
  subtleties in, 201
  switching behavior and, 292
symbols/symbolism
  in barrier pictures, 81
  in color, 9
  in fragmentation pictures, 62
  in induction pictures, 142
  interpretation of, 8-9
  in system pictures, 22, 298
  in threat pictures, 108
symmetry, 7, 73, 99
system pictures, 23-39
  abstract representation, 22, 39
  artmaking strategies, 41
  case study, 245, 246-48
  chaos in, 41, 42
  chaos pictures vs., 49
  characteristics, 17
  conceptual basis, 298
  flowers in, 33
  meaning in, 41
  newly-emerging system, 40
  representation of alters in, 25, 26, 27, 28, 29,
    31, 33
  representations of abuse in, 35
  self-image in, 23
  structure analysis, 22
  symbols in, 22, 298
  trees in, 29, 31, 35